ATM Business Startup

How to Make Money from Owning, Operating, Selling, and Marketing Automated Teller Machines – Step-by-Step Guide to Earn a Great Passive Income

By

Brent Connelly

Copyright © 2020 – **Valley Of Joy Publishing Press**

All Rights Reserved.

No part of this publication may be reproduced, stored in a retrieval system or transmitted in any form or by any means, electronic, mechanical, photocopying, recording or otherwise without the proper written consent of the copyright holder, except brief quotations used in a review.

Published by:

Valley Of Joy Publishing Press
Cover & Interior designed

By

Renee Robinson

First Edition

Contents

Introduction 10

A History of the Automated Teller Machine 15

The What, Why, and How 29

    What is an ATM, and how does it work? 29

    Why is owning an ATM a good business idea? 31

    How do you decide that you need an ATM at your business? 34

    How do you make money? 34

All About Automated Teller Machines 41

    What's in a name? 41

    Parts of an ATM 43

    Types of ATM Machines 46

The Legalities of Owning an ATM Business 51

    Regulatory Guidance 53

        Identifying ATM Operators or Owners 56

        Due Diligence for ATM Operators or Owners 58

        Monitoring of Activity 59

    New ATM Machine ADA Standards 61

ATM Processor vs. an Operator 66
   Transaction Processing Companies 67
      The Workings of the ATM Processor 72
      How the Processor Makes Money 73
      Choosing an ATM Processor 74
   ATM Location Operator 80
      Educational Requirements 81
      Certification Requirements 82
      Required Skills 82
      Employment and Salary Outlook 83
      How to Become an Operator 84

Kick-Starting the Business 87
   To Franchise or Not 88
   Develop a Business Plan 88
   Seek Necessary Financing 89
   Find Placement Spots for Machines 89
   Establish a Legal Entity 90
   Buy the Basic Equipment 91

- Cost of ATM Machines 92
  - Vault Type 92
  - Type and Screen Size 93
  - Note System 93
  - Aesthetic Allure 93
  - Type of Lock 94
  - Additional Features 94
- Sample Costs of ATMs 95
- Cost of Maintenance 97
- Where To Buy An ATM Machine 97
  - Kinds of Brands 98
  - Used Dealers 98
  - ATM Dealers 98
  - Placement Services 99
- Final Steps 100
- Programming and Installing ATMs 101
  - Installation 101
  - The Vaulting of the Atm 108

- Do it yourself. 108
- Get the owner of the location to vault the ATM ... 109
- Have your ATM processor restock your ATMs for you. 109
- Machine Maintenance 111
  - Stop Jams 112
  - Keep the Card Reader Clean 113
  - Offer Bills Valuing at $10 or Higher 113
  - Stock Cassettes Often 113
  - Clean the Touchscreen 114
  - Control the Temperature 115
  - Schedule Maintenance 115
  - Deal with Printed Receipts 116
- Steps to Reloading 116
  - Insurance Coverage 118
  - Withdraw the Money 118
  - Inside the ATM 119
- Conditions for Success 121
  - Location 121

    Safe Spot 123

    Outdoors 124

    Trial and Error 124

    Foot Traffic 126

Convenience 127

Being Available 129

Competition 129

Types of Suitable Business Locations 130

    Restaurant/Bar 130

    Concert/Sports Arenas 131

    Convenience Store or Gas Station 132

    Hotel 132

ATM Security and Challenges 134

    Security 136

    Physical Security 136

    Physical Barriers 137

    Video Cameras 137

    Update Software 138

- Challenges of ATM Ownership 139
  - Theft Risk 139
  - Fraud 140
  - Fees 141
  - Card Retention 141
- Marketing 143
  - What Marketing Achieves 145
    - It Grows 145
    - It Equalizes 145
    - It Sustains 146
    - It Informs 147
    - It Engages 148
    - It Sells 149
  - Asking a Business for a Spot on their Premises 150
    - Benefits of Having an ATM 151
  - Growing the Business 159
    - Use your ATMs as mini-billboards 159
    - Alter your ATM screens to suit your brand 160

Give away cash purchase incentives 161

Customer Care 162

    Happy Customers 163

    Happy Employees 166

    How to Make Happy Customers 169

    Handle Complaints Well 172

    Know Your Product 172

Blunders to Avoid When Beginning an ATM Business .. 174

    Miscalculating Capital 175

    Buying Used Equipment 175

    Overvaluing Cash Flow 176

    Establishing Low Margins 177

    Not Getting a Signed Contract 177

    Service Agreement Mistakes 178

    Poor Geographical Placement 179

    Not Establishing a Relationship with a Bank 180

Conclusion 181

Introduction

Today, we are asked for our PINs in every sort of retail store, on the Internet, and in libraries. Debit cards have grown into the de facto currency.

We can go to almost any country in the world with just a small card in our pocket, assured that we would gain access to money anywhere as far as Easter Island, Hong Kong, Paris, Giza, and even Antarctica.

All this is because of the near-total global integration of ATM networks.

Some machines now promote advertising by other companies while others enable users to buy airtime for their mobile phones, or work as Internet kiosks.

The quick distribution of real cash continues to be the most significant, transformative purpose of the ATM, even with all its digital innovations.

Now, people that use ATMs prefer making payments with cash to evade interest charges and credit card debts. Traders also prefer people that use paper money. Therefore, owning an ATM around their business helps business owners to decrease their credit card processing charges.

Therefore, it is a win-win for traders who either have or run their own ATM or who have a contract with an IAD to run one for them.

With my background in the business, I have experienced the advantages of investing in an ATM.

For this reason, I shall share with you the knowledge I have on becoming a free ATM owner.

People that own businesses should continuously be on the lookout for several alternatives to earn more money. These alternatives can range from brand-new commodities to policies aimed at increasing their sales. For this reason, many business owners look to using an automated teller machine as a good option for increasing passive revenue.

Brick-and-mortar businesses that may benefit from having an ATM include gas stations, restaurants, and nail parlors. Having an ATM can be very beneficial, in that it can lure more clients and earn the business more money.

How profitable is an ATM? Before we explore that answer, let me share with you a brief story of my experience and success in the ATM business.

I had spent several years in business and was doing well. Over time, I realized that most of my customers preferred using cash over their credit and debit cards. I would occasionally have a customer in need of an ATM. This made me curious, and I began doing some research on the possibility of owning an ATM.

I realized that, besides banks, anyone could own an ATM and make money from it. I did extensive research and asked other small ATM business owners many questions.

From my research, I found that owning an ATM is one of the best ways to earn extra money from my business. I also found out about ATM brokers who were remarkably fast in making responses. The brokers were very committed and spent lots of hours helping me with the research, responding to questions about the business, as well as finding the right contractor to help with the installation of the machine.

The help from ATM brokers was extremely important to me as I was brand new to the industry. Their help with the issues I had was so quick and efficient to me because any downtime is money out of my pocket. They were notably patient in responding to all of my questions that are typical for the industry. Their service was very remarkable and helpful.

If you are new to the industry, it is a good idea that you should first do research and inquire about people with similar businesses. I bought my first ATM for $1,500 and had it installed in my shop. It proved to be a good investment as it attracted more customers and earned an excellent passive income for me.

After around two years, I installed another machine. I realized how beneficial they are and started convincing other business owners to install ATMs at their businesses. ATM commerce did so well that I began fully focusing on it as a business.

In a span of seven years, I had installed several ATMs at different locations. In 2003, I sold the business for millions of dollars and started teaching people about the ATM business. I am confident that, with the right information, many people can reap many benefits from this venture.

A History of the Automated Teller Machine

Cash still reigns in lots of places. It is one of the things that people depend highly on a day to day basis.

Paper money has been used as the primary source of exchange in small and big nations and cities all over the world. It has been so for the last few centuries. For this reason, ATMs (automated teller machines) have become more prevalent than ever before. They enable access to money to be much more obtainable and convenient over time.

To get a clear understanding of exactly what ATMs are, I feel it is good to dig into the past and understand how they came to be. There is value in knowing the history of this technological development that has made banking easier.

The cash dispenser, as it was first known historically, came to be in 1967. This was the earliest concrete proof that retail banking was evolving. The ATM's introduction signified the rise of modern digital banking.

Various people can be accredited to the discovery and design of the cashpoint. Among them include Luther Simjian and Don Wetzel in the U.S and the U.K's own James Goodfellow and John Shepherd-Barron. There are also engineering companies like Asea-Metior, Speytec-Burroughs, Omron Tateisi, and De La Rue.

It was not easy to come up with this development. The ATM is a very sophisticated technology. There was never one particular eureka moment that marked its arrival.

The roots of the ATM harken back to the 1950s and 1960s, when stations, supermarkets, candy dispensers, automated public-transportation ticketing, and self-service gas were becoming popular in society.

According to an account by "*Pacific Stars and Stripes*," back then, the first cash machine seems to have been deployed in Japan in the mid-1960s. Little has been published about it ever since.

The most successful initial deployments took place in Europe. Bankers in the country responded to the rising cost of labor by engineers soliciting to come up with an after-hours cash distribution solution, as well as the increasing unionization of the banking system. This resulted in the Barclaycash, Chubb MD2, and the Bankomat in Sweden, in the U.K, which were three independent efforts. All of these entered use in 1967.

Thanks to a long chain of innovations, Cashpoints materialized after a couple of years. Steel, magnetic tape, plastic, video-display units, or the more recent Windows operating system made up some of the general nature of the machines.

In the 1960s, the earlier non-existent algorithm that incorporated an encrypted PIN with a customer account came about, as others were purpose-made, like the cash output mechanism. Active collaboration between engineers and groups of bankers contributed a lot to these components' development. Each of these endeavored to give solutions to various issues that were in the complex challenges experienced in the development of the ATM.

No electronic equipment had ever been so exposed to the components. Further automation was invited from the need for human intervention in early systems. For example, they could regularly run out of cash or jam-up. Sometimes they could give out a number of banknotes rather than of just one, by mistake. All this could occur without the owner's knowledge.

They were activated by paper tokens or plastic that would only be enabled by the operating bank, and in some cases, that specific bank location only. In some banks, the money would be kept in the machine until a later date when it would be returned by post to the customer. This would be done once the account had been debited.

For this reason, early ATMs were unfriendly, clunky, rigid, and standalone. They could only give out cash when stimulated by a token.

Due to these limitations, it is barely a surprise that it took longer than a decade for banks to put the cashpoints to use. Only a handful of experiments and a few tests here and there were done.

Back in the day, only a few people believed that the cashpoint would make a significant difference to the ordinary customer. In reality, this forecast may have appeared like a sure bet. This is because cashpoints came to be before debit or credit cards were a popular option to coins and bills, especially in a time when most of the world's citizens worked in a cash economy. Even personal checks were primarily limited to the wealthy, with the exception of France and the U.S.

It is easy in today's world of e-commerce and mobile banking to update the central records from the point of a transaction. However, cashpoint was one of the earliest devices to work with real-time networking.

In the early development of ATMs, devising a means to communicate with a central computer, and hence notify customers of their account balance, grew into a significant design interest. The Swedish savings banks started putting a networked cashpoint to test in 1968, in cooperation with IBM. This led to a collaboration between Lloyd's Bank and IBM.

In 1973, the bank stationed various networked machines in the United Kingdom. However, there was still a long way to go for widespread online authorization. IBM engineers produced the pipes and rails throughout the 1970s. They also came up with the standards on which additional components of the cash ecosystem, like point-of-sale terminals and credit cards, would ultimately depend on.

The invention of the modern ATM was a relief to many average consumers. It freed them from the long queues for services that had initially been limited to bank hours.

As the devices spread out over vast regions, this convenience unwaveringly altered the consumption patterns of customers, enabling impromptu dining and random shopping on the weekends. It simultaneously made it possible for retail banks to expand their base of customers. They did this by allowing access to customers who had earlier been banned from using a credit card or a store credit account.

Employees relocated away from teller services and into sales, thus altering the nature of work in bank branches. They also began to cut costs by decreasing office staff and shutting down branches when such sales shots failed to actualize. High-end products and services like investment funds, mortgages, car insurance, and credit cards, owe a debt to the outsourcing of conventional banking to ATMs. With the so-called "branch transformation" prevailing as a hot topic in the industry, this process remains even today.

ATM technology across the world has actively been shaped by bank regulators, who dictate who can operate and own them. They monitor where they can be physically located as well as the cost of withdrawals.

The ordinary person has influenced ATMs, too. The people have influenced the way the machines look, how they operate, as well as their position as a program for today's surplus of balance queries, transfers, and deposits. In some European countries, the airtime top-ups for pay-by-minute cellphones have also been incorporated into automated processes at ATMs.

A few years following the appearance of the first machines in Sweden and England, manufacturers were working in Japan (Omrom Tateisi), the U.S. (Diebold and Docutel), and Britain (Speytec-Burroughs). They mutually deployed cash machines across Canada,

Europe, Israel, Latin America, Cyprus, and in their home countries.

By the early 1980s, however, engineering companies such as De La Rue, Asea-Metior, Docutel, and Chubb, had neglected the industry as all declined in keeping up with advancements in electronics and computing. Some manufacturers, like Burroughs, had barely settled their objectives in deployment. Citibank went on using them in its global, established network until the 1990s and dropped plans to capitalize on its exclusive CAT-1 and CAT-2 devices.

It was not the same case with IBM, which possessed business contacts, engineering expertise, and the marketing muscle to be dominant in the market. Until executives embarked on deploying a new model—the IBM 4732 family—which were conflicting with earlier models, including the widely used and already-successful IBM 3624, the company appeared self-assured to overcome its competitors.

Several banks assessed the device and declined to purchase it. This was because IBM had turned the banks' earlier computer infrastructure's vital capital investments completely obsolete. This obsolete nature stretched inside bank branches past the mechanical devices to the software and machine that sustained communication across the bank's network. It even went to models for administered cashpoint networks.

The move IBM made unintentionally soured banks. This, therefore, opened the ATM market to new manufacturers of the cashpoint. As expected, IBM later entirely left the payment-technology systems.

Two companies based in Ohio - Diebold and NCR – were formed around this time, operating on technology that would empower them to control the stocks of cashpoints for the subsequent two decades. Following the fiasco that entailed the IBM 4732, NCR developed its trade on software that imitated the IBM 3624. In the meantime, Diebold and IBM came together and established a joint venture called InterBold. This was in 1984.

The aim of this venture was to unite IBM's global distribution system with the self-service technology of

Diebold's. However, the joint venture ended seven years later, in spite of growing sales. This was because IBM's returns did not reach its expectations, partly due to the increase in local processing structures, which had annulled IBM's plan to connect ATMs to its costly mainframes. Diebold had also not realized the international market breakthrough that it had hoped for.

Diebold and NCR were effective in transforming the cash-vendor dinosaur into the current multi-function and sleek ATM. The innovations by the companies involved a shift to giving out cash horizontally (which reduced jams), video display units that were customer-friendly, augmented functionality, including money transfers and balance inquiries, as well as buttons alongside the screen that were programmable.

NCR and Diebold were, however, never alone. An increase in the number of banks using ATMs all over the world saw a rise in the number of manufacturers:

- Fujitsu, Hitachi, Hyosung, and GRG, in Asia
- Honeywell in the U.S.

- Siemens-Nixdorf (today, Wincor), Olivetti, Phillips, in Europe

Large banks in Europe also generated proprietary networks that numbered in thousands of ATMs that were favored by the shared systems of U.S. banks. Their subsequent interconnection fees also approved of these ATMs.

ATMs continued to be a significant capital investment, notwithstanding changes in quicker methods of identifying unpaid accounts, modular manufacturing, and the associated decrease in costs of service.

The application of dedicated phone lines confined them to high volume non-bank locations and bank branches, like large airports and busy train stations. This condition eventually lifted with the industry's choice of the Windows operating system and the arrival of digital telephony.

These two modifications that seem simple transformed the ATM, enabling a combination of credit card authorization networks with past diagnostics. They also allowed revived growth in the deployment of the machine in the late 1990s and the arrival of the Independent ATM Deployer (IAD), who were ATM merchants unaffiliated with a significant financial institution.

But, the ATM industry is not as rosy as it seems. For instance, in 2014, in a move aimed at reducing costs, a reduction of the size of ATM fleets and the regularity of existing machines' cash resupplies was made by Chilean banks. They did so while promoting the application of cash remittance networks sponsored by the government in small retail stores. This transit led to campaigns against banks on social media and a public outcry.

There has been a doubt about the need to deploy ATMs in developing countries following the success of mobile banking in Africa. While limiting the substantial investment needed to install and manage established ATM networks, payments that raise the need for money and bank branches in rural regions, and mobile banking offering the opportunity to improve economic inclusion in Asia, Latin America, and Africa.

The future of remittances and mobile banking remains uncertain for many developing countries, despite the many advantages. The ATM has displayed pervasiveness for nearly 50 years, in its humble and uncertain beginning. But it was not until 15 years after the machine's invention, in the 1980s, that the ATM's progress was assured.

The What, Why, and How

Let us have a clear understanding of what an ATM is and how it works.

What is an ATM, and how does it work?

An automated teller machine (ATM) is an electronic banking outlet. It makes it possible for consumers to finish initial transactions without the help of a teller or branch representative. Most ATMs can be accessed by anyone with a debit card or credit card. However, some credit cards may have more trouble.

Any person can invest in an ATM - supermarkets, retailers, landlords, entrepreneurs, city authorities in need of an increase in revenues at parks, and other public places. Simply, anyone who can count money can own an ATM.

Getting into an ATM business is amazingly a very affordable investment. You can get any ATM model for under $2,500, inclusive of shipping. Failing to work with an ATM company with full experience in the business is what will cost you a lot. Learning from mistakes can cost you much more than the typical investment cost.

Before you begin, ensure that you find out who can operate an ATM. Many entrepreneurs and investors are allowed to invest or operate an ATM business. The only exception is if they have been involved in any sort of financial crime or an offense and have a criminal record.

Why is owning an ATM a good business idea?

The demand for ATMs by customers in businesses like service stations, convenience stores, malls, amusement parks, restaurants, office buildings, clubs, hotels, sports bars, as well as other retail locations is stable at the moment. Over time, the demand is only getting stronger. More massive crowds of people in need of fast and convenient access to cash are typically attracted to such locations. More withdrawals from the ATM are made in the busier spots. This brings in more income for the ATM owner.

If you do not have your own location, you can begin the business by investing in the machine and placing it in a merchant's store. Ensure that you make an agreement to have a share of the surcharge fee. This way, you can ensure that you earn from the machine, as well as increase the business owner's interest in the machine.

Also, having an ATM around the business will attract more consumers. This shall, therefore, lead to more profits for the store.

Not only is adding an ATM affordable for business owners, but they also require little maintenance or attention from the business owner. Owning an ATM would be beneficial for you and the business owner whose location you are using.

Your money is recycled daily, and the funds expended by the ATM are transferred electronically to your account within one or two days. This then brings about a tangible profit on investment.

You will never experience a rise in business expenses. Best of all, you will not be required to hire employees to monitor the operation of the machine. There is also no time commitment.

Businesses make most of their money through an ATM when people use an ATM and pay a small fee between $2 and $3. This is the simplest way to conceptualize earning a commission from the ATM. For this reason, when a business allows an ATM to be installed at their spot, they have a chance to make something from it through commission.

The business owners, however, typically do not receive the entire commission. If the ATM has been rented, the business that maintains the machine by filling it with cash, doing repairs, amongst other maintenance activities, receives a share of the money.

The split in commission varies depending on several reasons, but the business makes money based on the overcharge proceedings.

Although businesses can earn money through the fees, some business owners look for additional methods of using the ATMs to make more money and decide to run advertisements on them.

Some companies usually place screens on top of ATMs and sell space for adverts to run on the machines. This, therefore, increases revenue for the locations and ATM operators.

How do you decide that you need an ATM at your business?

It is essential first to determine whether you can justify the expense accrued on an ATM. This is because the cash machine costs thousands of dollars. You should fully contemplate having an ATM bank machine installed if your business meets any of the following criteria.

- Clients often ask where the most next ATM can be found.
- Transactions in your business are reliant on cash.
- A number of people walk by your business daily and can spot the ATM itself or a sign for it.
- Your business makes various credit card deals for small amounts.

How do you make money?

There are many ways that an ATM owner can create a wealthy income from an ATM business. From owning and running an ATM machine or two, you could make an income from interbank interchange and surcharge fees. This is made easier if you are dealing with a transaction processing company, as we will discuss in a later chapter.

ATMs could also earn you an extra income opportunity when you sell advertising on the screen or on the outside of the ATM.

As an ATM business owner, you may be the ATM operator. In some cases, an ATM could belong to another individual, financial institution, or a group of people, and you are the one to operate it. This can entail you handling any issues to do with ATM services, loading it with money as a vaulter, or doing the balancing of accounts and general operating of the business. This could earn you a decent income.

After gaining vast experience as an ATM operator, you could help other owners with parts and service, and also offer them help with cash vaulting services that deal with the loading of cash in the ATMs. You could also provide other ATM owners getting into the business with services in selecting suitable locations and the technical know-how.

ATM operators and owners can charge the ATM users (cardholders) a surcharge fee for doing a transaction with their ATM. With an ATM, you have the capacity to charge this fee on the basis that you are giving your clients a service that is convenient for them.

You are offering the customers the chance to save time when they want access to money from their bank without the stress of traveling all the way to the bank. ATM owners usually charge a fixed surcharge fee during the process of setting up. Normally, they receive a percentage of the charges imposed on the customer.

When you connect an ATM customer to a significant bank, the banks that issue ATM cards (aka issuers) usually pay a certain amount of fee to the ATM. This fee is known as interchange.

The interchange fee varies depending on the banks and networks of operations. All the operating fees used by the ATM business are usually generated from this fee. Normally, depots dealing in ATMs take a percentage of the money that is leftover and later distribute them to their clients depending on the number of transactions, as well as the kind of location. In some cases, the extra fee that customers of some ATM depots usually receive $0.05 to $0.15 above their surcharge.

With adequate traffic around your location and a good number of customers using your ATM, you can be guaranteed of beneficial income generation, which you get to keep as the owner.

To get the surcharge fee, you have to work in cooperation with a good processing center. Most will share the revenue you earn as per the instruction you give them as the ATM owner.

Some of them can share the revenue with five other persons who contribute to your ATM business. Such people could be the cash loader (vaulter), retailer, location owner, ATM owner, or investor.

Here are some examples of surcharge income:

- Surcharge amount could range from $2.00 per transaction
- The income per use could be around $2.10
- An average of five uses a day amounts to $10.50
- In thirty days, the amount may sum up to $315.00, which may later amount to an annual sum of $3780.00

More often than not, the person purchasing the ATM gets to set the surcharge amount for using the machine. This surcharge usually varies from one business to another.

For a fast-food restaurant, convenience store, or another standard retailer, this cost can range from $1.50 - $2.00. Some bars and nightclubs will set the fee at $2.50 or more. Prices at adult bars, specialty shops, and other casinos can reach $5 or more.

Keep in mind, however, that if you set the convenience fee too high, nobody will be interested in using your ATM. The cost of convenience gets too much if it crosses a certain point. From my experience, if you charge anywhere between $1.75 – $2.50, your machine will make money.

With the average ATM transaction being around 180 processes or so per month with an average ATM fee of $2.50, you can do the math and see for yourself and see how much you could potentially earn.

When you ensure that your ATM is located in a busy area, the surcharge alone will earn you an average income of $450 per month.

I have suggested 180 transactions for this scenario because that is the aggregate number of transactions done on many of the machines. You could find machines with fewer, and some with lots more.

The slowest machines may have 60 to 90 transactions a month with two or three a day. Busy machines may, however, be used around twenty to thirty times a day. This would amount to about 100 to 600 transactions per month.

Do the math and see for yourself. The busier the location, the better and faster your income and wealth grow from the business.

All About Automated Teller Machines

The popularity of ATMs has steadily been on the rise since the first ATM appeared in 1967. Across the world, more than 3.5 million ATMs are being used.

What's in a name?

They are also known as "bank machines" or "automated bank machines (ABMs)" in different parts of the world. There are two basic kinds of ATMs. In the basic units, customers are allowed to receive updated account balances as well as withdraw cash.

Besides the name "automated teller machine" as used in the United States, ATMs go by a variety of names. In Canada, the name automated banking machine (ABM) is used, although the term "ATM" is commonly used in Canada, and in several Canadian organizations. The terms cash machine, hole in the wall, and cashpoint, are most popularly used.

Several ATMs have a symbol above them displaying the possible networks to which it can connect, and showing the name of the organization or bank that owns the ATM. In most cases, the ATMs that are not operated by a financial institution go by the name "white-label" ATMs.

The more sophisticated machines report information on an account, aid in line-of-credit payments, transfers, and accept deposits. A user must be an account holder at the bank that runs the machine for him or her to obtain the high-level features of the advanced units.

According to analysts, ATMs will become even more accessible in the future. They anticipate an increment in the number of withdrawals done at ATMs. In the future, ATMs are expected to be full-service termini instead of or a supplement to conventional bank tellers.

Parts of an ATM

All ATMs contain the same essential parts, although the design of each ATM may be different:

Keypad: The keypad permits the customers to key in information like the type of transaction he or she intends to do, the amount of the transaction, and the PIN.

Screen: This contains the ATM instructions that lead the customer through the process of executing the transaction. Notices are also conveyed on the screen — for instance, the balances and account information.

Cash dispenser: Money is given to the customer through a slot in the machine. The slot is connected to a vault at the base of the ATM.

Printer: When needed, customers can demand receipts that are printed by the ATM. The receipt notes down the account balance, the sort of transaction, as well as the amount of money involved.

Card reader: This is the part that reads the chip on the magnetic stripe on the back or the front of the card.

When using an ATM, customers are required to use a plastic card for them to complete a transaction. These plastic cards can be either a credit card or a bank debit card. For authentication, consumers are also required to acquire a personal identification number (PIN) before they can use the card to complete any transactions.

Usually, these cards come with a chip that aids in the transference of data from the card to the ATM. These transmissions work like a bar code, which is also scanned by a reader suited for decoding codes.

In various cases, credit unions and banks own the ATMs that their clients use to do cash transactions. But, companies and individual people may also purchase or hire ATMs through an ATM franchise or by themselves. When small businesses or individuals like gas stations and hotels own ATMs, the model of profit is based on the fees paid by the users of the machine.

Although banks own ATMs with the intention of making profits, they additionally intend to use the convenience of the ATM as a service that they provide as a tool of attracting clients to them.

Providing ATMs also takes some of the burdens of customer service from bank tellers, thus saving the banks' money in staff payroll costs.

ATMs also make it less complicated for travelers to gain access to their savings or checking accounts from almost anywhere they are in the world.

When they use international ATMs, they get a more favorable exchange rate than they would at many of the offices where a currency exchange is done.

Also, making use of an ATM is less strenuous than cashing traveler's checks. It arguably makes travel more secure, as the traveler is not required to carry a lot of cash.

Nevertheless, the bank that the account holder deals with may impose a certain percentage of the amount exchanged or a transaction fee.

Many of the ATMs do not record the exchange rate on the receipt, making the tracking of money spent challenging.

Types of ATM Machines

Automated teller machines can be split into the following categories:

Countertop ATM

Countertop ATMs are made for those businesses that do not have sufficient space for a freestanding cash machine.

Freestanding ATM

This ATM is a popular option for a business with plenty of floor space. Normally, they are about two by two feet in size.

There should be room enough for customers to stand. Such machines are usually found in convenience stores, restaurants, and gas stations.

Dial-up ATM

These ATMs need a dedicated phone line as most cash machines use a 56 kbps modem to dial into an ATM processing network.

Wireless ATM

Businesses that already have a high-speed internet connection, as for credit card processing or a WI-FI hotspot, can make use of wireless technology for an ATM also. This lends versatility for a cash machine's position on the premises.

Built-in ATM

A built-in, also known as through-the-wall ATM, is the kind of cash machine usually located at banks. They are typically more pricey to install since they need construction work to install. If your business has outdoor, substantial foot traffic after hours, the built-in cash machine may be a reliable choice.

However, bear in mind that there are heightened risks from thieves.

The Legalities of Owning an ATM Business

Over the past number of years, the number of privately owned ATMs has risen. The reasons vary from one party to another.

ATMs bring about a substantial revenue for their owners and need little time to maintain. Additionally, they are accessible to customers of the business to get money.

Although the ATMs may be profitable to their owners, this can indicate a heightened hazard to the bank serving the business owner. There is also a risen risk of money laundering associated with the machines.

For this reason, there are several administrative terms and conditions put in place by the government for the owners to observe. This is for any owner with one or a hundred machines. Cash from criminal ventures can be used to fill the machine as a means of cleaning the money. The customers using the ATM launder the money by making withdrawals of the criminally-acquired cash in the ATM. The clean money is later sent to the ATM operator or owner's account via ACH deposits to seal the deal.

For this reason, the government has come up with regulatory guidelines to ensure that the business is conducted legally and that no customer falls prey to illegal businesses.

Before looking at the regulations, let us have a look at some regulatory guidelines that some people have given as solutions to some of these risks involved in the business.

Regulatory Guidance

There is an administrative expectation that all ATM owners or operators must perform when applying for a business permit.

The FDIC (Federal Deposit Insurance Corporation) deals with anti-money laundering.
https://www.fdic.gov/regulations/examinations/bsa/manual.html

The FFIEC BSA Examination Manual (https://bsaaml.ffiec.gov/manual) states that banks need to come up with procedures and policies to deal with the perils connected to Independent Sales Organizations (ISO) consumers.

These procedures and policies should aim at including appropriate tools or methods of monitoring suspicious activity, as well as due diligence. At the very least, the systems and strategies should be inclusive of:

1. A survey of state databases to distinguish inherent queries or concerns with the principal owners or ISO.

2. Storing documents showing the locations of ATMs that are privately owned and judgment of the ISOs target geographic market.

3. Proper due diligence on the ISO that is based on risk by a review of permits, corporate documentation licenses, references, or contracts.

4. Anticipated account dealings, including currency withdrawals.

5. Proper comprehension of the ISO's authorities for arrangements of currency servicing for clandestinely run ATMs, including the origin of replenishment currency.

6. Recovering data from the ISO concerning the due diligence on its sub-ISO systems, like the volume of transactions, the location and number

of the ATMs, source of replenishment currency, as well as dollar volume.

Banks should also accomplish due diligence on ATM owners, very appropriately. The due diligence might be inclusive of:

1. Ascertaining the sorts of businesses in which the ATMs are placed, capturing the addresses of each ATM location, and recognizing the targeted demographics

2. Analyzing state databases for information on the ATM proprietors.

3. Evaluating licenses, corporate documentation, contracts, references, or permits, including the deal of the ATM transaction provider.

4. Determining the origins of currency for the ATMs by evaluating copies of lending agreements, armored car contracts, or any other documentation.

5. Ascertaining the anticipated levels of ATM activity, including withdrawals of currency.

This, therefore, means that banks should implement and grow a process of identifying the owners of ATMs, as well as obtaining adequate information on due diligence to give them the ability to rate the risk for the customer and create a system meant for monitoring.

Identifying ATM Operators or Owners

The first step that banks can use to manage ATM operators or owners is to recognize which consumers have privately operated or owned ATMs. There should be a clearly set out means of identifying them for account opening, as well as the current customers.

When it comes to account opening, the CIP checklist should add a plan to recognizing those customers who have personally owned ATMs. They can do so by inquiring of the customer. To protect existing customers, there should be a means to distinguish ATM owners.

To do this, the easiest method is to do a review of ACH reports for deals coming from known ATM servicers. For instance, common ATM servicers include:

- RBS
- FDRetail ATM
- Worldpay
- FirstData
- Coredata
- CDS
- Datastream
- Cash Depot
- Elan FS
- Cardtronics
- SWITCH
- Metabank
- EFUNDS
- FDC Star System
- MVNT

A customer is likely to be an ATM operator or owner if they are receiving ACH credits from these originators.

Another way is to pay customers who are more likely to have an ATM onsite a visit. Such customers may include restaurants, convenience stores, bars, bowling alleys, and gas stations. You will be required to investigate who operates or owns the ATM if they have one onsite.

Due Diligence for ATM Operators or Owners

Once the Bank has identified an ATM operator or owner, it should gather extra data to reach a conclusion about the ATM operator/owner, as well as the ISO or sub-ISO. The most effective method of obtaining the information is to directly get in touch with the client to gather the data.

Obtaining this information about the ISO or sub-ISO, as well as the ATM owner's procedures, will help the bank gain more knowledge on the ATM business and help in dealing with the owner or operator.

The bank should have a copy of the contract, Name of the ATM or ISO network they have contracted with, the account number that the ATM transactions flow through, if unknown, the whole numbers of ATMs owned or run, as well as location of each, amongst many other factors mentioned earlier.

After obtaining this information, the bank must then do a thorough review of public databases to discover if the ISO or principal owners have any issues with the state. They can simply accomplish this by looking for information via a web search.

Monitoring of Activity

After the bank has obtained sufficient information, it should complete a process to watch the accounts of the ATM owners. The amount of control required, as well as the frequency, is determined by the information obtained during the due diligence process. Every ATM owner needs a different kind of monitoring as one size does not fit all in this case.

Monitoring should be inclusive of an examination of all the business activity of the customer as well as every activity at the ATM. The control is made almost effortless if the action that takes place in and out of an account is associated only with ATM activity.

The number of cash withdrawals and reimbursement for transactions (credits) must relate to one another. Further investigations should be done on any significant variances to ascertain if it appears appropriate and reasonable.

If more than ATM action emerges through the account, then monitoring can prove to be a bit harder. It can, however, be accomplished by linking cash withdrawals to ACH credits.

Monitoring should always be performed, even if the customer provides the ATMs with proceeds on the property, which can make the process more difficult. For a present client who has obtained an ATM lately, there should be a decreased level on the number of cash deposits. This is because the cash is going into the ATM. Given the kind of trade the customer has, the amount of ACH credits linked to the ATM should be reasonable.

The risks connected to ATM operators or owners can differ from one customer to another; they must be adequately addressed. Monitoring can cease by making a comparison between regular activity and the current activity.

This can only be done once the predicted activity is ascertained. Any modifications should be additionally reviewed and documented.

The regularity of monitoring should be restricted to the risks identified as well as the bank's appetite for risk. To meet the regulatory expectations, the monitoring styles, and the actual monitoring that is done must be documented.

New ATM Machine ADA Standards

A recent law concerning ATMs has been passed under the Americans with Disabilities Act (ADA). It went into effect on March 15, 2012. These brand-new ADA standards demanded full compliance by the deadline date of March 15, 2012.

If you are an ATM company, a retail merchant operating one or many ATMs, or an ATM owner, these new requirements will touch each terminal in a retail location or your ATM portfolio.

I am going to talk to you about the things you ought to know about these recent changes and the way they affect your business.

From March 15, 2012, consumers with disabilities began finding the process of using an ATM much more comfortable than ever before. From March 15th, it became a must for ATMs to be in compliance with these new ADA requirements, regardless of whether owners agree with them or not.

Some ATMs may need you to make a number of enhancements, making it easier for your customers to physically access and interact with your ATMs. The following are some of the new requirements and design standards.

Clear floor space: The space in front of the machine is required to equal 48" x 48", which is 16 square feet.

Height and Reach: The required reach to the top working button changed from a height of 54" to 48". This has helped ensure that customers can comfortably reach the input buttons of the ATM. Drive-thru ATMs are, however, an exception to this change.

Voice Guidance: To be of excellent service to visually impaired customers, all ATMs must be speech enabled. A female jack of 3.5mm must always be available for headphones.

Accessible route: For accessibility of wheelchairs, one side of the clear floor space with no obstruction must be close to an open route or a different open floor space leading to the ATM and adjoined to the clear floor space in front of the ATM.

Function Keys: Function keys must be devised to provide a visual contrast to their background surfaces.

Display Screen: Characters displayed on the screen must be in San Sarif font to ensure visibility from 40" above the center of the floor in front of the ATM. They must contrast with their background and also be a minimum of 3/16" high.

Input device: Essential surfaces must be elevated above the surfaces around, in that input device controls are tactically obvious.

Numeric Keypads: Keypads must be designed in an ascending or descending design. The clear key should be marked with a raised left arrow, the enter key with a raised circle, and the cancel key must be marked with a raised X. The key meant for decrease value should be labeled with a raised minus sign, whereas the add value key must be labeled with a raised plus sign.

In case your spot has a number of ATMs, the most convenient ATM must adhere to these new 2012 ATM rules and regulations. Nevertheless, the law dictates that the terminal inside a place and one outside the same place be viewed as two separate positions. Both must be compliant in cases like these.

Braille Instructions: Instructions on a braille to aid in the voice guidance feature mentioned before must also be implemented.

ATM Processor vs. an Operator

Automatic Teller Machines (ATM) were usually only accessible at your bank. This was until recent years that you see an ATM at every turn.

Although it is somewhat owing to the success in profits that is very evident from the ATM owner, it is also a win-win for the relationship between the merchant and consumer. An ATM grants the customers access to cash right from their private bank account when they need it. No more trips and long queues at an out of the way bank.

It provides their consumer with cash flow for purchases if the retailer at the ATM area is a retail store. Very advantageous for the customer, don't you think?

Ultimately, the owner of the machine also has a flow of passive revenue because of the little convenience fees that accumulate from each transaction. If the bank directly manages the ATM you use, then it is obviously directly linked to the money in your bank account.

In the case of an ATM being owned by a separate third-party, the ATM processor presents the link needed between the customer and the money in their bank account.

Transaction Processing Companies

A transaction processing company is often a third party company that is employed by a retailer to manage operations from several channels like debit cards and credit cards for retailers that are obtained from the banks. Usually, they are split down into two kinds: front-end and back-end.

Front-end processors hold links to supply authorization and settlement to the bank merchants as well as several services card associations. As for the Back-end processors, they allow transactions from front-end processors. For instance, The Federal Reserve Bank moves the funds from the issuing bank to the dealer bank.

In a process that usually lasts a few seconds, the transaction processor will verify the details obtained by rerouting them to the particular card association or card issuing bank for verification and also do a sequence of measures aimed at fighting fraud against the transaction.

Further parameters include the country where the card was issued and the history of the previous payment. These are used to assess the possibility of the transaction being authorized.

The information will be transmitted back to the merchant through the payment gateway, once the payment processor has received proof that the details of the credit card have been verified. The merchant will then execute the payment transaction. If the card association denies verification, the transaction processor will deliver the notice to the retailer, who will then reject the deal.

In America, there are transaction processing companies that give their merchants access to their ATM processing data at any time of any day. Clients in these companies are served with the most advanced technology in ATM processing.

An example of such companies is Columbus Data Services. Some of these companies are enrolled with all ATM networks like Pulse, Visa, Star, Honor, Switch Commerce, MasterCard, Discover, Quest, and Novus.

With a transaction processing company, you can be sure of the completion of all operations in one cash transaction without flaw. Sometimes, an error on hardware could occur in the course of a transaction leading to non-dispensing of the cash. In such cases, the transaction processing companies "nullify" all of the progress of the transaction and return the accounting system to how it was before the transaction processing began.

After the transaction operations are successfully completed, the transaction processing company is cleared by the transaction-processing system, and the cash is paid to the customer.

ATM clients are granted their own data tracking website for their ATMs. It gives them the ability to analyze and monitor their ATM data at any time, which includes the status of terminal, transactions, cash levels, and more.

The system also enables printed and downloaded ATM reports and statements, including every day, monthly, and dispensed amount, annual cash balances, transaction summaries, and more.

Clients can access the online ATM portal from any mobile device using phone apps that are available for both iOS and Android devices. Some companies also provide a 24/7 customer support line that is toll-free. This is in case the clients should ever need help with the processing of the ATM.

If a holder of a card uses the ATM and complains that the ATM did not give out the accurate amount of money, most companies have a toll-free number that can be used any day throughout the year to dispute any transaction.

The ATM processors also render a valuable service for banks. The bank saves a staggering amount of money, time, and human resources since the machine provides cash directly to the cardholder, thus no need for interaction with a human teller.

If a banking institution owns the ATM, there is a straight connection between the holder of the card and the money in their account. If a third-party owns the ATM, the ATM processor renders this connection between the cash and the customer.

The single transaction the consumer observes is, in fact, an intricate network of data exchange between customers' bank account and the machine. This process is done with the help of a host processor.

The ATM processor transfers data between the machine and the customer's bank. Just like with the cell phone service, it can be likened to the relationship between the service provider and phone. You can opt to choose a different provider and still use the same phone.

The Workings of the ATM Processor

Behind the scenes, the first thing that the ATM does is to access the customer's bank account. After the customer inserts the card and enters his or her personal identification number (PIN), that particular information is transmitted to the ATM processor. After that, the processor forwards a request of the transaction to the issuer of the card.

The processor affirms that the funds are accessible for withdrawal and then generates an electronic funds transfer (EFT) from the processor's account and the bank of the customer. Once the transfer of the funds is officially done, the ATM processor gives the machine an approval code. This grants the machine the permission needed to administer the requested cash amount.

In the end, the customer walks away happy, but the ATM processor is still working actively. A while before the close of the following business day, the ATM processor will convey the funds into the ATM owner's account from the customer's bank account. This compensates the owner of the machine for the money that was given to the customer.

How the Processor Makes Money

Self-supporting ATM processors earn money by charging a small fee on every transaction. It is known as an interchange fee.

A lot of institutions and banks are okay with paying this small fee since the automation and convenience still save the bank money by not paying a teller for the transaction.

Often, the interchange fee is passed on to the owner of the ATM. This is the reason behind some ATM transactions listing two service fees. The owner of the ATM will transfer the interchange fee on top of the convenience fee if they are responsible for the ATM processor's payments.

It is essential for an ATM owner to look for processors that do not charge late fees. With free ATM processing, you are not only guaranteed zero processing fees, but also the provision of the most protected network, the most dependable machines, as well as a more distinguished level of customer service.

Choosing an ATM Processor

Whether you have machines already or are just beginning your ATM business, your ATM processor has a significant influence on the long term success of your business and profitability.

For this reason, understanding how an ATM processor is chosen is very crucial for current ATM owners and also those looking to change ATM processors. The fact that the ATM processor transfers the money to the right account on time is not enough. You need an ATM processor that is going to present ongoing assistance and support exceeding the simple processing transactions.

If your ATM processor responds to your call for help by telling you that they only send money where it needs to go, ATM setup and programming, then you will struggle on your own. That is totally not helpful. Your ATM processor should be more than a service provider. They should be the right business partner.

To get a clear understanding of what services your ATM processor should offer, below is a list of what your processor should do for you. This will help you when evaluating the ATM processors.

Some things that an ATM processor should do are rather obvious. However, there are distinctions, even with the essentials.

Automated Payments

It is obvious that your ATM processor ought to transfer your funds to your bank account. Nevertheless, it should actually be more straightforward than conveying money on your bank's website from your checking account to your savings account.

First and foremost, these ATM payments should be automated. If not, you should at least have the alternative to make the automated payments on your ATM. This business is entirely about generating and growing passive income. If you have to admit transfers yourself, it lessens your passive income.

The automated payments may appear to be like small yams. Yet still very important when it comes to choosing an ATM processor that renders a service that runs by your business goals.

Sales of ATMs

A company can run entirely as an ATM processor. But, there is still an advantage to working together with a processor that also trades the ATMs. If you get one or several of the machines from your ATM processor, then they can process the transactions using their service.

Hardly will you find an ATM processor selling an ATM that is incompatible with their service. It does not even make sense. A processor that also trades the machines is especially helpful. This is mainly if they sell used or refurbished ATMs. You can be guaranteed tools at a better price, without the pain of possible issues of compatibility with your ATM processor.

Payment Splitting

Sometimes you may be required to send payments to multiple accounts for some reason. It could be because you have numerous accounts to deal with different expenses. You have a business partner with a separate account or any other purpose. Your ATM processor could make it easier for you to split your payments.

Though it is possible for you to split those payments all by yourself using online banking, this makes your income system less passive.

For this reason, have a keen look at the payment processing choices offered by your ATM processor, and ensure that you are operating with a processor that is going to assist you in growing an ATM business that meets your goals.

Shorter Contracts and Low Fees

In your search for an ATM, you may find ATM processors that sell brand-new ATMs at an impressively low price. It will definitely seem like a great deal at first. However, a lot of companies that give generous discounts for their ATMs usually envelop a lot of fees in the services that they provide. At first, you may save a few hundred. But, over time, the ATM processor will get that discounted amount of money back through fees charged on services.

Often, dealers that earn money from slightly higher fees will need a contract of 3 to 5 years. When a deal lasts longer, the requirements ensure that the fees cover the cost of the discounted ATM. The prices may end up being higher than the original discount you got on the ATM if you sign a 5-year contract.

The opposite is the case for ATM processors that sell their ATMs at slightly higher prices. Their services usually come at the lower fee structure. Also, these ATM processors often provide shorter-termed contracts that range from 1 to 3 years. They typically offer these shorter contracts since they do not need to make up for the cost discounted on the ATMs.

For this reason, examine the contract requirements and fee structures of the potential ATM processor and reflect on how much the fees are going to cost you over the contract's lifetime.

Flexibility

Lastly, support and flexibility are significant. Your ATM processor should be easy to work with and responsive. If your ATM processor cannot get you the help you need, when you need it, then there isn't much help they are adding to your business.

It is best if you can get the support of your ATM processor any time, any day. You may need random help with the machine, any time. It is hard to tell when. For this reason, your ATM processor's support services should be available anytime.

Your ATM processor should be less a service provider and more of a business partner. Responsiveness and availability are essential in getting this kind of cooperation from your ATM processor.

ATM Location Operator

An automated teller machine (ATM) operator, also known as an ATM repairer or servicer, is a person who diagnoses, services, and installs ATMs.

ATM field operators go to the locations of their clients to identify and fix problems on-site. They also uninstall the machine and return it to the shop where ATM bench technicians will work on it.

Operators use equipment like multi-meters, hand tools, and diagnostic software to fix problems such as cash dispensing systems that are malfunctioning and worn card readers. An added number of ATM technicians will be needed to operate electronic kiosks as the financial industry develops new technology.

Educational Requirements

Some workers at the entry-level are required to have attained an associate's degree, although many ATM technicians hold a high school diploma.

This associate's degree may involve courses such as microprocessors, programming fundamentals, calculus, and electro-mechanical systems.

Postsecondary education in fields applicable to this career may be attained at a vocational school. In such schools, students learn the basics of transistors, circuits, and ATM mechanics.

The great majority of entry-level employees learn practical training on the job. Despite the electrical knowledge that a candidate may have when hired, the training may last several months, depending on the specific machines they will be working on.

Certification Requirements

Manufacturers usually have a particular interest in candidates who carry additional certification, like the one granted by the International Society of Certified Electronics Technicians (ISCET).

Also, the Electronics Technicians Association International (ETA) offers 80 plus certification programs in various electronic specialty fields.

Required Skills

The following are the necessary qualities for ATM technicians, as reported by the U.S. Bureau of Labor Statistics (BLS):

- Analytical and creative problem-solving skills
- Dexterity, considering technicians must operate in odd positions

- Knowledge and experience in information technology
- Strength to lift heavy stuff
- A professional driver's license
- Good communication skills

Employment and Salary Outlook

The median year-long income for all ATM, office-machine, and computer repairers was $37,710. This was as of May 2017, as noted by BLS (Bureau of Labor Statistics).

Although the demand for servicing on weekends and holidays could end up in opportunities for overtime work, most of these operators were employed on a full-time basis.

These workers' employment is anticipated to decline in a couple of years slowly.

This is because the demand for ATM repairers may fall due to an increase in the use of electronic mobile and computer-based banking.

How to Become an Operator

Keep a clean criminal record. Due to the kind of job, an ATM operator has access to huge amounts of money in the course of their day to day activities. But, if any inconsistency with an ATM balance occurs, the employee will be at risk of termination of contract and prosecution. For one to be hired at any business, you will be expected to undergo a thorough reference and background check.

Get a high school diploma or equivalency. To get the training needed, you will be expected to verify that you have obtained a diploma or a General Educational Development (GED) certificate or a diploma. Typically, this is usually the least educational qualification to join a technical training program. Some exclusions may, however, be made for individuals who have not achieved an equivalency certificate but may be highly talented.

Register in a mechanics vocational program. These programs can be found in some specialized high schools and most technical colleges. In order to undergo training about ATMs, you will be required to hold a primary comprehension of mechanics.

It is advisable that you also possess an associate's degree. If you desire to seek an associate's degree, contemplate on an associate's of installation and repair, or applied science. If a bachelor's degree is your main interest, think of electronics or mechanical engineering.

Get a certificate of ATM repair. Look for a vocational school program or community college that has a course in ATM repair. Contact vocational schools to get information about the best course plan.

Register in a private ATM training course. A number of organizations, like TestLink Services Ltd and ATM Gurus, usually offer ATM repair training for $800 to $1,000. This training session lasts for 1 to 3 days. Ensure that these courses offer a certificate and are approved.

Apply for a job with a firm that provides on-the-job training or an ATM manufacturer. This is the best option for those who already have some mechanical training.

Before the job begins, you will be assigned to a training session. After that, you will earn a certificate and start working with similar kinds of machines that you were taught to use.

Apply for a job with an ATM manufacturer or an ATM repair company. Several banks contract out their ATM maintenance to these organizations. By being employed by such companies, you are more likely to secure a regular job.

Freelance your skills as an ATM repairman. Some individuals in the industry work based on a contract. After gaining several years of expertise and outstanding employer recommendations, you can begin your own ATM repair business. This way, you can freelance or retire in peace.

Kick-Starting the Business

Once you have the know-how on starting your own extraordinary ATM business, you can get a means to generate an almost passive source of income in the long-run.

This is the primary reason that automated teller machines in public locations can make someone a good profit. However, make sure that you follow the steps required along the way before getting engaged with this kind of business.

To Franchise or Not

Determine if you desire to begin your own company or to become associated with an ATM franchise.

Many franchises are available dealing with ATMs at the moment and may sell you the machines that you need and a name brand.

While it can be more costly than directly buying some ATMs by yourself, the franchise option presents you with a proven business plan.

Develop a Business Plan

After you have made a decision between commencing with your own self-governed business or buying a franchise, pen down a business plan. Your plan should include fiscal predictions, information on critical roles in your company, as well as industry and market research.

Seek Necessary Financing

Once you have a business plan, you can start approaching lenders and investors. If you decide that a business loan is in your best interests, contact the Small Business Association office in your area and ask for information about SBA loan providers.

Find Placement Spots for Machines

Find places where you can place your ATM. For this, you ought to search for unrestricted areas with a large amount of regular foot traffic.

For instance, you may anticipate around 3 to 5 percent of the people who walk by your ATM would use it. You can then approximately calculate the amount of money you can make from a location per month as well as annually. You can guesstimate transaction fees of $2 to $4 per instance.

It is advisable that you approach and talk to several business owners and form an arrangement to install your ATM on their property. You will most likely pay some sort of commission or rent to the business owner.

In the following chapter on "Conditions for Success," we'll explore location selection in detail.

Establish a Legal Entity

The legal features of your ATM business are very crucial. For this reason, come up with a legal entity before beginning the business.

If you intend to do business under a business name, it will be necessary that you register it with your county clerk. You may also desire to establish a business entity so that you can evade any peculiar liability.

An example of such a business entity could be a limited liability company. To achieve this, you can file articles of organization with your state and afterward pay the relevant filing fee.

The purchase of a business license from your city or county government is also a requirement.

Buy the Basic Equipment

Purchase the equipment required for your ATM business. You could acquire several machines right from the start, or you may desire to begin with just a single ATM and expand later.

Prices may vary greatly depending on the design of the machine you get, with each ATM estimated to cost anywhere between $3,000 and $10,000.

Your expenses will definitely not end there. You may likewise be required to purchase some additional equipment, like a clip that you can use to refill the machines with money.

Sometimes, you may also require a vehicle that you can use to move the ATMs around, as well as service them.

Cost of ATM Machines

Select an ATM with the features that you desire. The typical range of an ATM is in the $2,500 to $3,000 range. With a $2,000 to $8,000 budget, you can be guaranteed an ATM of any kind.

Here is a list of the key features that you need to consider when contemplating on what machine you desire for your ATM business.

Vault Type

There are generally two types of vaults: Level 1 and Business Hours. The challenge of breaking them and the strength of their walls are the main distinctions between them.

Level 1 is created to hold cash safe every hour of every day, whether guarded or not. Business hours, on the other hand, are designed to keep money when someone is guarding it.

Both vaults weigh about 300 lbs or more. Their steel can endure 50,000 psi in physical force.

Type and Screen Size

Screen size tends to range from 10 inches to 15 inches. They can be either touch-enabled or not. Larger screens and touch screens will cost more.

Note System

The main thing about the note system is how many cartridges it holds and how many notes it can carry. Larger cartridges and more cassettes make for easier and fewer refills.

The cheaper machines generally use a 1,000-note drawer. The high-end devices can get up to 8,000 notes carrying multiple cartridges.

This option will depend on the volume you believe you will be holding.

Aesthetic Allure

How modern does the ATM look? That is a significant determinant of cost. For a lower-end system, you can go with a small model. For those providing the service to more affluent clientele like resorts or hotels, you may consider going with a sleeker design.

Type of Lock

There is a whole range of lock options, from S&G locks to standard electronic locks. S&G produces a one-time order that is time-specific and updated.

Cencon is the ATM locks gold standard. It includes elements like encrypted computerized keys, unique sequences, internal source of power, dual token access control, and alarm connectivity. If you are considering using a service to load the machine, you will possibly desire an upgrade to a system based on software-based Cencon and S&G.

Additional Features

The details above cover the basic features of the ATM. Other elements you will need to think about is a price that you will not change later, whether the ATM is built-in or free-standing and language support.

Sample Costs of ATMs

The information below will give you a clear understanding of the costs associated with ATM. If a cash machine seems like a suitable investment for your business, you could acquire a device in the ranges below.

- ATMs have a general cost of around $1,000 up to $25,000 plus.
- A through-the-wall ATM (also known as a Built-in ATM) can be acquired at a rough cost of $5,000 to $10,000 and above.
- A freestanding ATM costs an approximate cost of $3,500 to $7,000 and above.

- An ATM lacking a cassette and a dispenser can be bought at around $1,250 to $1,750.
- A refurbished or used ATM can be purchased from a start-up cost of about $500.
- An 800-note cash drawer Triton stand-alone ATM with door sticker, dial-up connectivity, dial combination lock, and lighted sign fetches about $2,000 to $2,500.
- A through-the-wall/ built-in ATM with a 2,000 note cassette, thermal receipt printer, wireless capability, and monochrome LCD goes for around $6,000 to $9,000.
- A freestanding ATM with dial-up connectivity, 1,000 note cassette, thermal receipt printer, and a color LCD, may cost $3,000 to $4,000.

Generally, customers all over the nation are said to buy an ATM for a standard cost of $2,000 to $4,000. There are additional ATM costs that one might include:

- ATM vendor fees. If included, it could cost around $10 to $20 per month.
- Cash loading service. Though optional, it may cost roughly $40 to $60 per trip.

- Replacement receipt paper.
- An extra cash cassette. This may cost approximately $100 to $500.
- A phone line which may cost $20 to $40/month.

Cost of Maintenance

When buying an ATM for your business, you need to consider the cost of maintenance. Fortunately, ATMs come with a 1-2 year warranty on parts.

Some companies also extend an ATM service team that can regularly take you through most repair issues. Nevertheless, to be on the safe side, it is wise to make an annual budget of around $200 – $300 for repairs or maintenance of ATMs.

Where To Buy An ATM Machine

Where you buy your machine is a significant factor that you should consider. There are many dealers in the market with all sorts of ATMs.

For this reason, you should be careful about the company you choose to buy from. Where you purchase the machine will determine your mode of acquiring it. It could be leasing, going to use a placement service for turnkey transactions, or even buying it outright altogether.

Kinds of Brands

The leading brands for small business ATMs include:

- Genmega
- Triton
- Nautilus Hyosung

Used Dealers

If you are considering going for the companies dealing in used ATMs, there are sites that focus on used ATMs. Some also sell both new and used. Below are a couple of online sites where you can get used ATMs.

- Craigslist(Find your local Craigslist site)
- ATMTraders (https://www.atmtrader.com/)

- eBay (https://www.ebay.com/)

ATM Dealers

To find dealers with both new and used ATMs, below are a few examples of places you can find them:

- EverythingATM (https://www.everythingatm.com/)
- http://atmequipment.com/
- ATM Link(https://www.atm-link.com/)
- National Cash Systems (http://www.nationalcash.com/)

Placement Services

Services provided for installation will give an utterly significant solution. In turn, they retain most of the surcharge revenue but give you a cut of a certain percentage. Here are a few examples you could lookup:

- CORD Financial (http://www.cordfinancial.com/)

- Lieberman Companies (https://www.liebermancompanies.com/atms/)
- ATM Network (https://www.atmnetwork.com/)
- Prineta (https://prineta.com/)

Final Steps

The last three steps will be explained at length in the next few chapters:

- Set Up the ATMs
- Consider Payment Processing services
- Evaluate How to Vault or Restock the Machine

Programming and Installing ATMs

The ATM will be shipped and dropped from the manufacturer directly to the address listed on your application after you lease or purchase a new ATM from an ATM depot unless other arrangements are made.

Installation

Many companies are supplying certified refurbished ATMs if you are interested in buying one or owning several. The ATM will be shipped from the ATM processing partner with prior programming and ready to use. All you need to do in the installation process is to bolt the ATM to the floor, plug in the power and the phone line, and allow the customer to use it.

When it comes to the physical installation of the ATM, you can do it yourself, or plan for the ATM to be installed for you professionally by a certified ATM professional. I highly recommend installation from a professional.

The programming and setup of ATMs is the part where many ATM owners have totally no experience and knowledge.

It is, therefore, vital that you operate your business in liaison with an ATM processor who grants instructions programming and setting up of your ATMs.

It is also crucial that you can build a good rapport with your ATM processor and call for free when stuck and need some help with the ATM.

Some substantial amount of money is lost every day your ATM is not functioning. For this reason, it is vital that your ATM processor is always there to assist you in dealing with challenges that may arise in the setup process. This will still get your ATMs up and running at all times.

Another option would be using a technician sent by your ATM processor to install an ATM in a new location for you. Of course, this will not come for free. But, when your new ATM is in business, it will save you a lot of time and headaches.

This option can be a considerable way to get some ATMs up and running as you learn the ropes of ATM programming and setup. However, just like the ATM vaulting service, it may not be necessary for you to use your ATM processor's setup service.

An ATM is basically a steel safe that is UL rated. The machine dispenses money and typically weighs 150 – 250 pounds or more.

The rating from Underwriters Laboratory is included in most ATM's as "UL 291." It is different from a UL rating for heavy-duty safe or gun safe. Its rating is a Business Hour Vault. Its basis is on break-in time.

Ensure that your ATM is leveled and bolted to the floor. When it comes to the best stories for security, concrete floors are the best. If the floor is made of thick concrete, consider getting underneath, through to the downstairs ceiling to bolt it.

Hidden at the bottom of the ATM are four or more pre-drilled holes that are used for positioning the machine. Installers typically use redheads, which are individual concrete anchors (or a similar product) to bolt down the ATM.

After it is well positioned, the ATM is then secured into the regular 110V / AC terminal and connected to a dedicated phone line. If you attempt connecting the

ATM to a shared line, a PBX phone system, or a fax line, you are most likely to suffer transaction issues.

Issues could range from reversals, delays, chargebacks, non-dispense issues, and incomplete transactions. Install a separate phone line and spare yourself the headache of problems that may occur in the future. If your ATM is equipped with the capability to process the internet, you can also use your internet service.

If you are interested in training on how to operate your ATM, lots of companies arrange for that during installation and help you through it at no additional cost. They can walk you through the new programming once your ATM is installed.

Once that is done, the ATM is ready to fill the machine with $20s or any pre-selected amount of money you set during the settings process. Some places may prefer that you dispense $10 bills, as it can be very advantageous.

An ATM cassette typically holds 700 – 1500 notes. However, you may never need to use that much. In case you ever do, do not fret. You could call that a functional problem. Think of it this way, one thousand notes of $20 bills compounds to $20,000. Good problem, don't you think?

On average, an ATM retailer puts in thirty to forty $20 bills per day. That makes up about $600 – $800. Considering the ordinary ATM does eight to ten transactions in a day, with an average withdrawal of $60 per transaction that computes to about $480 – $600 per day.

You can keep removing your currency every evening if you are the operator or owner. Otherwise, as the ATM business owner, you can alternatively load the machine weekly.

Check the company's free online monitoring system to ensure that you do not have too little or too much cash.

For higher counts of transactions, you can fill your ATM with $10, but they are a little more laborious to get from your bank or cash register. It can be harder to get them since you need to request for the notes at least two days before filling.

They also do not dispense as well because they are not new $10. They are used more often and get worn faster. Usually, twenty-dollar bills are easier to find at banks and more unique.

You can dispense more than one denomination if you want. However, to do so, you need a machine that uses various cassettes. A single cartridge is standard on most machines. You can purchase a second one as another option. You can get conventional ATMs with two cassettes at high-end retailers.

For the continuous running of the ATM, all you need is the phone line or internet service, a receipt paper, a few dozen $20s, and clean power. Do not share the power with coolers, refrigerators, compressors, freezers, or any other devices that demand high power voltage. Just like a cash register, put money in every morning and take it out every night. It does not take long — only a minute or two.

There are a few keys that you press to run your totals and balance out. Remember that there is also an online monitoring system that you can use to check your reports and balance. All the cash that was withdrawn from your ATM is deposited into the checking account of your business. The income that you earn from the surcharge monthly is then deposited at the end of every month.

The Vaulting of the Atm

It is common knowledge that it is vital to keep your ATMs stocked with cash. This will keep your business humming.

Now, when it comes to vaulting of the ATM, you can use the following options:

Do it yourself.

Yes, you can. Just get the money and take it to your ATMs to stock all your machines again. This is the most beneficial method of vaulting your ATMs as it does not attach any extra cost to your business.

If you choose to restock your ATMs yourself, your ATM processor will be quite handy and convenient if his monitoring services regularly inform you when one of your machines is low on funds.

Get the owner of the location to vault the ATM.

Since the business owner is frequently there, this can be a good option for vaulting often. Maybe every day.

For this option, the location owner shall also have an absolute concern about the safety of the ATM since the cash they are stocking it with comes from their register. In addition, this option minimizes your workload.

It is without a doubt that the owner of the location will want to be paid for their labor. Nevertheless, the expense is often worthwhile.

Have your ATM processor restock your ATMs for you.

This option totally takes the duty of vaulting your ATMs off your plate.

Whether you use this service from your ATM processor or not, this option is worth the consideration. As your business grows, you may own ATMs in locations that are challenging for you to reach and refill yourself, or you may need the services of an armored truck to guard your money. The best option may be having your ATM processor vault your ATMs for you.

Usually, this service will not be free. It is highly likely that your ATM processor will charge you for this service. This cost is the primary determinant of whether or not you may use your ATM processor to vault your ATMs. However, the service should be fair-priced in that it does not kill all your profit. $1.00 per transaction may be a manageable and reasonable price depending on the service done. Either way, ensure that the cost is suitable for your ATM business model.

In the long-run, you may not need to use the vaulting services of your ATM processor. However, working with one that provides ATM vaulting services can be beneficial in the expansion of potential locations for your ATMs, as well as decrease the workload of always restocking the ATMs with cash.

Machine Maintenance

Owners of ATM businesses should regularly do routine checks on their machines to make sure that they are working correctly, as required.

In order to avoid downtimes, ensure that you have an alert service. With the service, the ATM will send you a text message whenever the ATM is used. Ensure the machine is continuously kept stocked with enough cash in ideal increments.

You can also use online monitoring services to keep constant checks to confirm if your ATM has enough money. Routine inspections should also include external parts for any signs of wear and tear, checking the machine's hardware, as well as updating the software.

When an ATM has established itself as a consistent, reliable, and steady machine in a particular place, individuals learn to trust it. Once they do, they will be loyal customers and give their business to that machine any time they are in need of banking transactions or fast cash. This ends up being a win-win situation for both the customer and the ATM business.

In this business, you can invest just a few thousand dollars and earn a few hundred thousand every single month. With the right strategy and the right location, you can receive 10%, 20%, or even 60% on your investment from owning a successful ATM business.

Stop Jams

To prevent future difficult bills that may bring about jams, sort out the money before loading the ATM. A large number of the jams in ATMs are brought about by poor currencies. When sorting out the money to be loaded in your ATM, the following faults are what you should look for.

- Torn bills
- Soggy bills
- New bills

- Taped bills
- Dogged eared bills

When you remove these kinds of notes from the bunch that you are to load, you will manage to lessen the cases of jams in your ATM.

Keep the Card Reader Clean

When you keep the magnetic head of the card reader clean, it is essential that the information embedded on the card of the customer is read properly.

For this reason, clean the magnetic strip of your card readers once every week. This way, you get to avoid misreads.

Offer Bills Valuing at $10 or Higher

It is a known fact that ones and fives get used on a regular basis. This means that they swiftly turn into the "difficult" currency that I mentioned earlier in point number one. When you use currencies of tens and above, your ATM will have cleaner currency, thus giving customers an easier time when using the ATM.

Stock Cassettes Often

As many say, when you plan properly, you prevent future poor performance. Failing to plan is planning to fail.

For this reason, plan ahead, especially before the use of the ATM at peak time, like weekends and holidays. This will help you avoid running out of money, which, if you do, your customers will not have the best experience.

Clean the Touchscreen

Your ATM will be used by customers from different kinds of places, and with different kinds of professions. Such professions could range from a mechanic, a farmer, or even a chef. All of them stop by your spot to use the ATM. Well, it is obvious that your screen will quickly get all sorts of dirt.

When the dirt, sweat, and grease accumulate on the screen, the sensors of the ATM may be affected, making the screen less quick to respond to touch or even stop working. This will definitely cause a customer to be a less satisfied customer, thus a loss in the profits of the company. To effectively get rid of the debris and dirt from the screen, use a microfiber cloth to clean the screen daily.

Control the Temperature

Some environmental conditions the ATM is in can damage or lessen the performance of your ATM. This could be moisture, humidity, cold, or excessive heat. Such conditions not only affect the customer, but also the interior electronics, belts, and rollers. Kindly note that the proper operating temperature should be as close to room temperature or 72 degrees as possible.

Schedule Maintenance

When you get an ATM service contract, ensure that it is inclusive of scheduled service for preventive maintenance. If the contract does not include this, it is advisable that you take a second look at your service provider.

You can schedule regular preventive maintenance during a time when your business is slow.

The ATM's mechanical parts like belts and rollers that wear out or breakdown over time need proactive replacement before they fail. This will, in turn, reduce customer care issues greatly.

Deal with Printed Receipts

Receipts that are generated digitally may grant you a chance to talk to your consumer even before the transaction.

An organization can encourage frequent ATM visits by potential or current consumers by simply working with vendors on printing deals specific to financial institutions or generate distinct deals for ATM users.

Steps to Reloading

These are some of the most frequently asked questions about the ATM Machine business.

People are often curious and want to find out exactly how one loads an ATM Machine with cash.

As mentioned earlier, the amount of money much an ATM Machine holds very much depends on the kind of ATM Machine and the cash cassette you are using.

There are ATMs with a fixed cassette which cannot be removed. They are generally in lower end ATMs designed for locations with a low volume of people. They can also be upgraded when making an order for the machine.

There are also the ATM Machines with removable cassettes. They come with all kinds of configurations from small sizes like the Triton TDM, to the Mini-Mech ones, and multi cassette machines that are suitable for multiple denominations

If you are currently in the process of building up an ATM network or are operating a single device, it is possible that you may need to keep your costs down by restocking the machine with the cash yourself. Before you do so, you will need to ensure that you have enough insurance in place and have the know-how on how to load your machine.

Insurance Coverage

Verify that the insurance for your business covers you as you carry the amount of money needed to withdraw from your bank to reload your ATM.

Read through your insurance plan's policy documents and get familiar with anything excluded in the papers and is related to carrying the cash. It would be a good idea that you be accompanied by another healthy person or more to transfer vast amounts of money. If you leave any money abandoned anywhere, you will almost unquestionably revoke your policy and end up losing the ability to make a claim for any losses incurred.

Withdraw the Money

Establish the amount of money you need to withdraw from your bank to recharge the machine. Note down the amount that you take out on your records.

Go to your bank and withdraw the needed cash. Go back to your machine immediately when you have the money you want. Try to reload your ATM after you can lock the premises for privacy purposes.

Inside the ATM

Open your ATM and pull out the reject tray and cash cassette. Verify that the reject tray is emptied. Your ATM's reject tray is meant for the crumpled and dejected notes that cannot be dispensed. They are generally diverted into the reject tray. Note down how much cash was rejected in your record books.

Review the bank notes that you have and make sure they are free of dog-ears, tears, or any other defects. Such flaws can cause the bills to be diverted to your machine's reject tray. After checking through the banknotes, open your ATM's cash cassette.

Slip the money into the cash cassette while ensuring that they are appropriately positioned.

Close the reject tray and cash cassette, lock them, and carefully put them back into the ATM.

After locking the machine, follow the instructions on the screen that help ready your ATM for use. Every ATM make and model varies in the way these readying instructions are carried out.

Conditions for Success

Location

Having an ATM business is like any other kind of business. However, location is a very crucial factor in the ATM business. Owning an ATM at your event or company is much like real estate whose three most essential elements are location, location, and location.

You most certainly need a state of the art machine that has the kind of features that you want and is appealing to the eye. But, all that may not be of much use if you do not have that ATM at the right location.

Some business owners choose to place their ATMs in a dark corner where it will not use too much space that could be used for other activities. They treat their ATM like an illegal product that needs to be kept out of the public eye.

Regrettably, doing so makes your ATM effectively unnoticeable. Your customers may not realize that it is there, and worst still, they could even forget that it is. For consumers to put the ATM to good use, it must be visible to them, if possible, exactly in their pathway.

In your efforts to put the machine in a spot that will make it highly convenient and visible, do not obstruct traffic with it. Doing this alone could be the most significant move you could ever use to draw more clients to your ATM.

You are required to place them in the right place to reap the maximum benefits of owning the one ATM, or several ATMs. When putting together an effective ATM placement strategy, here are a few things that you ought to keep in mind.

Safe Spot

Just as it is with the real estate sector, safety is a critical factor that you should not ignore when it comes to the placement of ATMs. After all, people are not going to use it if they do not feel safe while standing at your ATM.

With this in mind, you ought to ensure that your ATM is in a space that is wide open and well lit. Also, do not place it in a dark corner as people will not feel safe while withdrawing money from it.

For a user to feel safe, he or she needs to be capable of seeing everything surrounding him or her in all directions.

When your ATM is in a spot close to some sort of apparent security system or a security camera, it will encourage your customers to feel at ease and secure while carrying out a transaction with your ATM.

This is definitely what anyone with an ATM would desire to be the case.

Outdoors

For several firms, possessing an outdoor ATM is a factor to take into account. Doing so makes the ATM available for people to use 24/7, instead of it being open to people only during regular business hours.

This can be very beneficial for the business as it can aid in the increase of revenue earned from the ATM. The caution you should most definitely have in mind, in this case, is that security is all the more critical.

An outdoor ATM ought to not be in a space that is anywhere near where a potential thief could hide or far from corners. It should also be well lit, even at night. Additionally, the installation of a security system and a camera would be a very necessary requirement when having an outdoor ATM.

Trial and Error

Probably the most significant matter to recognize when it comes to the placement strategy of an ATM is that the whole process is that of trial and error. A lot of businesses will have a number of viable alternatives for installing an ATM.

Normally, it is in the best interest of the companies to give every location a try so as to be certain which spot brings about the best of results. Look at it as a sort of market research.

Before making a decision on which strategy is the best, you ought to put out a few options into trial first.

Marketing is a strategy, and since ATM placement is basically a marketing tactic, running a test is the significant step that will lead you to perfection.

Within your business, there could be a number of noticeable spots where an ATM would work well for you.

Try the machine in each spot for a few weeks at a time. Over time, you will be able to pinpoint a couple of spots that are suitable, and the ATM machine could be put to maximum use.

Foot Traffic

A number of businesses make the blunder of placing their ATM in a corner. It is as if it is a pain to the eyes and needs to be hidden away from the people. This may later prove to be a mistake because if people cannot find the ATM, they cannot make use of it.

If they cannot use it, then you will not see the advantages of owning one. It is imperative to have signs pointing people toward the ATM. It is even more essential to have the ATM in an area that is known to have a lot of foot traffic. You should, however, ensure that the machine does not block traffic within your business premises.

It often makes a lot of sense to place an ATM near the doorway or in the lobby, depending on the size of your store or business. This is not very often the ideal spot for smaller stores since it can block the entrance to your business.

Nevertheless, if the space in your store is enough for the machine and it is possible for a number of customers to make a line behind it, then this can be an excellent approach to maximizing the foot traffic near your ATM. In much bigger and more spacious buildings with a number of ATMs, one should always be close to the entrance.

Finding the right location is crucial for you if you desire to sell a particular thing in your store or want to be successful in your business. The ATM business still values this aspect. You need to find the right location in order for people to use it.

Convenience

Convenience is also very vital in the current fast-paced business atmosphere. Customers more often than not favor and approach the businesses that make it possible for them to enjoy convenience.

A good example of businesses that cater to convenience includes self-pump gas stations, drive-thru car washes, or fast-food drive-thrus. All these businesses, as well as other kinds similar to them, make it possible for customers to come in and out of the premises fast, all while taking pleasure in the service or product that they need. The same case applies to businesses dealing with ATMs and the customers that get services from them.

Any time customers need cash fast, they search for the closest ATM to withdraw some money. They seldom will go to a great extent to find an ATM. They are also more predisposed to withdraw cash from a machine that is available even during times when they do not need it right away. This is due to the habits of some customers that always crave convenience. For this reason, it is advantageous for owners of an ATM business to come up with such opportunities to provide services to customers as much as they can.

Since convenience is a big bonus for an ATM business owner to make available to his or her customer, other additional critical measures should be included in the owner's business plan for it to be fruitful.

Being Available

Ensure that your machines are in areas where people search for, need, and desire the services of an ATM. Simply, a place with high traffic.

Do not place the machines in an area that is off the main traffic-ways or hard to reach. Whether on foot or a car, the area should be comfortable for the customers to arrive. This helps attract them to your business, too.

Competition

As long as your ATM does not have the highest fee, it is okay if there are other ATMs in that area. Your ATM will still be in use if it is the most convenient.

Resist the idea of placing the ATMs in retail stores that are slow and traffic is less than 100 people per day. Also, avoid locations or stores whose customers can get money back at the register quickly with a debit card purchase.

Types of Suitable Business Locations

In premises with a large number of people coming in and out the door every month, as well as a need for cash, then you most likely to have the right spot for an ATM placement.

If lots of your customers keep asking about an ATM, that is also a good sign that your premises may be a good location. If your business area is not as busy and there is no such "requirement" for cash, then you should probably consider looking for a better location.

Good businesses to partner with might include:

Restaurant/Bar

More often than not, people will opt to make payment for expensive meals at restaurants using a credit card. They will do so to avoid needing much cash.

But, for many less formal places where the use of checks is probably a little lower, ATMs will most likely be used by customers. Also, several bars are highly likely to do several cash transactions.

For this reason, when an individual wants to stay a little bit longer than anticipated, they need to pay a visit to an ATM to withdraw some fast cash. Also, such spots get a lot of foot traffic even when people do not need the money to make payments for their meals.

Concert/Sports Arenas

People are highly likely to spend a lot of money when making visits to any sort of entertainment venue, whether they are buying souvenirs or meals.

Prices at any sort of entertainment arena are often way more elevated than what people usually expect. Not to mention, this venue is ideal for heavy foot traffic.

For this reason, they are forced to pay a visit to the ATM to withdraw more cash. Also, installing an ATM in an arena gives you a bit more openness to change when a time to raise the cost of using it comes. This can be quite helpful to you when making a little extra money.

Convenience Store or Gas Station

These two businesses are perfect for an ATM as they are filled with people using cash as a means of payment and are very much similar.

In some states, gas stations have begun providing their customers with lower prices for those paying in cash. This, in turn, makes an ATM very necessary.

Also, customers at the two places might find themselves buying items on impulse, thus spending more than they expected. This, therefore, forces them to pay a random visit to an ATM near the business.

Hotel

Very few businesses get more foot traffic than hotels. This fact alone makes the hotel a perfect location for an ATM.

Persons who are far from home will not have the ability to visit their bank and pick up more money. For this reason, they will visit the nearest ATM, which is likely in the lobby of a hotel.

Big hotels may even place an ATM on every floor. There is, therefore, a definite high need for ATMs inside such hotels.

ATM Security and Challenges

In the United States, ATM crimes are on the rise. Especially since several ATM deployers have yet to update their terminals to debit cards and EMV, which are issued by American financial institutions.

EMV is a payment method based upon a technical standard for smart payment cards. It is commonly referred to as a "chip card."

Most deployers still hold a mag stripe, which can be easily counterfeited. General threats involve high-tech attacks, like card skimming, and smash-and-grab raids. ATM deployers in the US are also starting to notice more explosive attacks and ATM Jackpotting.

One of the best ways to secure sensitive information and cash is to be familiar with your ATM terminals. This is according to a current whitepaper, *Improving ATM Security*. This is because an expert technician holds a more favorable opportunity of spotting malicious and compromised hardware on a unit.

The installation of ATM terminals can have an influence on security, too. Requesting for a criminal activity report from the region's law enforcement before installing the ATMs can make spots much safer for potential customers. This is according to the LAPD's ATM Safety and Security Tips.

Places that are more protected for consumers are also more reliable for the owners of the ATMs.

The report on criminal activity can be quite handy in determining the kind of security that best suits each location.

Security

As perils to ATMs develop, so do security measures enacted. To ensure ample security at your ATM terminals, explore the following security measures that you can use as suitable alternatives.

Physical Security

A lot of attacks happen at the top cabinet, where the ATM is most vulnerable. It is where the dispenser and mainboard connections are housed.

Managing key access and upgrading locks is a robust way of restricting unapproved entrance to the terminal. The power of alarms at ATM access points will inform staff at the site that the terminal has been breached, thus providing another assurance of security.

Investing in monitoring solutions or security management software with remote diagnosis allows ATM operators and owners to monitor and manage terminals in real-time. Security software comprises of features that scan for an unusual transaction or activity of service at each ATM. They then send alerts when suspicious activity is recorded.

Physical Barriers

Install bollards or concrete pylons to form a physical barrier around the ATM. These security standards help prevent smash-and-grab attacks and are designed to provide high levels of impact, as well as prevent damage to free-standing ATMs and store-fronts.

Additional real deterrents involve ATM body armor that encloses the terminal in anchor kits and steel plating.

Also, bolting the ATM to the ground gives an extra cover of security. This is because most anchor kits are intended to resist high impacts.

Video Cameras

Installing surveillance cameras helps protect both the ATM deployer and customers, thus acting as a crime deterrent.

Video cameras can be connected to monitor the ATM on the terminal, the area surrounding the terminal, or at the site. Even when thieves wear masks, hoodies, or other face coverings, the video cameras can still serve as identifiers for local law enforcement authorities.

The proper blend of technology and prevention strategy can significantly reduce the risk of theft at ATM terminals.

Update Software

The gradual shift to EMV has given ATMs in the U.S. away to a variety of cyber-attacks and has made them prone to criminal activity. Installing security patches and software updates on time are vital to guarding the terminal's operating system against illegal downloads of skimming software and malware.

Constant updating of access passwords and keeping employees and technicians with access to the ATM closely monitored, adds another layer of security.

Challenges of ATM Ownership

The first automated teller machine in the world was set up in London in a Barclays Bank's branch in 1967.

ATMs have made getting money more convenient, easier, and quicker for customers. However, this convenience comes with a plan.

Usually, ATMs do not possess the same attributes that humans have. With them, you will not have the same experience as when you have a financial institution full of people dealing with clients.

When you encounter difficulty, a machine will not be like an employee that you can talk to. Also, ATMs incur costs of security from theft and fraud. In the case of both, these felonies would leave both the owner and the customer frustrated.

Theft Risk

If you go to a bank, you're likely walking into a secured area watched by multiple cameras or a security guard. Those elements encourage would-be thieves to keep their distance from the bank.

You'll find no such security blankets with an ATM. It also takes a little time to take a card out, insert it in the machine, access your account, and get your cash. That can be enough time for a crook to attack, which is why some people won't use an ATM after dark or in secluded locations.

Fraud

Criminals have all sorts of scheming ways of getting through the devices, sometimes fitting small cameras and skimming devices to ATMs.

The machines usually record details of accounts and identification numbers of different people. Felons use these details to take out cash from the different accounts.

The U.S. banking system paid around $350,000 a day or $1 billion each year on ATM skimming. This is according to reports by the Secret Service.

According to the director of product management for Fiserv's Financial Crimes division, Mike Urban, "ATM skimming had reached "epidemic" levels and continued to grow."

Fees

Machine owners and banks usually take up a large amount of money from ATM transaction charges. Normally, ATM users can withdraw money for free from the ATMs belonging to their bank, but typically have to pay to withdraw money for a fee. This may make customers resort to other means of transactions to escape the fees impressed on ATM users.

Card Retention

People are used to ATMs giving. But the devices can also take. Just like any other device, they can breakdown and not be there when you need them.

There have been cases of some ATMs retaining any card if its owner fails to enter the PIN correctly after several attempts or keeping cards that are damaged.

An ATM user may normally retrieve his or her card if it has been retained by the machine owned by the user's bank. But, if the card is "swallowed" by your ATM, you can never be sure that the client can ever see it. This will, in turn, bring about a great customer care hurdle that will need a lot of attention.

Marketing

Effective marketing is the cornerstone of growing and maintaining your business.

Sometimes, marketing is thought to be the same as the advertising ways and means that companies apply to attract and bring in more prospective clientele to a business. However, marketing entails a lot more than brochures, online ads, newsletters, promotions, or websites.

The actual goals of marketing are to determine and satisfy the needs of the customer as well as determining the particular markets to trade goods and services to.

Marketing is defined as "the process of planning and executing the conception, pricing, promotion, and distribution of ideas, goods, and services to create exchanges that satisfy individual and organizational objectives." As per the American Marketing Association. Therefore, to carry out successful marketing, you should find your target market and understand what the market wants. Advertising is just one of the steps in a marketing plan.

Setting up an ATM at your business grants current customers with a significant and indispensable service. Everybody holds their time in high regard, and the convenience presented by an ATM gratifies the need of your customers to save time.

There are several fundamental business functions that stem from a good marketing plan that any small business would benefit greatly from. Let me first highlight a few significant reasons why marketing is very vital for any business in these modern times.

What Marketing Achieves

It Grows

For the growth of your business, marketing is a critical aspect. While your latest customers must always be your chief priority, efforts in marketing can assist you in expanding your customer base.

Limited exercises, like email campaigns and social media posts, can retain not only current customers but also inform new prospective customers about the product. Essentially, marketing ensures the future of your business through current and past engagement with customers.

It Equalizes

Marketing in these modern times is less expensive a game than ever before. Email campaigns and social media platforms have made it easier and more pocket-friendly for businesses to reach out to customers.

For small and medium enterprises, smart marketing can help you play the field when competing against competitors that are bigger and leading in the industry. Actually, marketing might even give small and medium enterprises a lift.

Because of the more modest essence of their businesses, leaders of small and medium businesses usually have more opportunities to give attention to each client exclusively through the numerous platforms of marketing.

Contemporary customers appreciate experience above pricing. Therefore, this sort of one-on-one intercommunication may propel clients to your business over more prominent companies.

It Sustains

"Marketing is more like food than it is medicine," according to Forty.

Primarily, marketing is intended to maintain the presence of a company. It should not be a solution to a loss of commitment.

With this in mind, marketing is a factor that businesses ought to organize and run every single day to sustain a good and wholesome relationship with their customers. Since it allows companies to keep an ever-present and long-lasting relationship with their consumers, marketing is very valuable. It is an open-ended plan that propels companies to flourish, not a one-time fix.

It Informs

Marketing is beneficial for customer education on a core level. You definitely understand all the details regarding your product, but the same does not apply to your customers.

For them to purchase your product, your customers ought to have a stable and reliable knowledge of the stuff it does and its workings. Marketing has been known to be the most powerful tool to express the position of your worth to your customers in an exciting and fun way. If educating your customers is on your list of priorities, then so should marketing.

It Engages

Engaging with your customers is the core of any thriving business, especially for small businesses. When you do marketing, you resolve the issue of how to keep communication running after your customer walks out the door of your premises.

Previously, a lot of interaction between business and customers was made up of face-to-face interactions. You walk in the hotel, talk to the host, smile at the waiter, etc.

As much as this face-to-face interaction is still very much alive, it is no longer the only way to maintain a relationship with customers. Customers need to be engaged continuously, even after they have left the business premises.

Marketing is, therefore, used to achieve this purpose. Whatever tool you use, you can transfer content with regards to the company to your customers and keep them interested beyond hours at the store. Your customers need to build a connection with your brand. Marketing is the best tool to do just that.

It Sells

As you have realized by now, without marketing, you can have no sales. It is essential as it assists you in selling your services and product.

The bottom line is, any business aims at making money, and marketing is an essential course to take to reach that top goal. Most marketers believe that without marketing, various companies would not be in existence today.

This is because marketing is the ultimate force that drives sales. You most definitely ought to have the right product; however, if people do not even have a clue about what you offer, then you will barely make any sales.

Small and medium businesses are required to generate brand-new, enticing content that will help them attract customers and drive them to purchase a product.

Marketing is helpful in sales, and sales, in turn, helps your business grow.

Asking a Business for a Spot on their Premises

Once an individual owns an ATM, he or she already knows the advantages that their machines bring to the business. Possessing a suitably positioned ATM does not just benefit the customers that use it. It additionally serves the businesses that host it.

Nonetheless, recognizing how relevant your ATMs are is not enough. You are also required to have the ability to explain the gains to business owners and acquire the permit to install your machines in their locations.

So what aspects will help you convince them to allow you to place the ATM at their location? Well, the following points can be very helpful in explaining the benefits.

Benefits of Having an ATM

So, what benefits do ATMs really have?

In short, customers view an ATM as not only a convenience but also as a necessity. ATM cash dispensers have become the most requested service in America and the fastest-growing device.

In the beginning, only banks operated expensive lease line ATMs. Locations obtained the ability to capitalize on the advantages of placing an ATM on-site when low-cost dial-up ATMs were introduced.

Develops Traffic

With an ATM at your location, you are likely to attract more consumers when you allow them to do both shopping and banking at your location. From walk-by traffic, ATMs bring about constant traffic at the store. When clients learn that a location has an ATM, they may opt to do their businesses at your shop, instead of going further to other locations.

If you are an ATM owner, but the location does not belong to you, traffic would still benefit you. More traffic would mean more people using your ATM, thus more earnings for you.

Grows Sales

The benefits of an ATM will yield more fruits if you own the location at which the ATM is installed. Typically, ATM customers spend more than a non-ATM customer by 20-25%.

From this, your place will get an increase in customer spending. The money generated through the ATM can be seen mostly in your daily register receipts, including the average sales. ATM customers take out $60 on average for every operation.

You can also add to your sales by using coupon options on your ATM as well as on-screen advertising. They usually increase collateral sales dramatically, too.

When you offer these significant services, you will experience a noteworthy lead over your competitor.

Brings about a Competitive Edge

As you know by now, ATMs are very convenient devices for human beings. The more services you offer to your customers, the happier you make them. Providing services customers expect in turn builds up loyalty in employees.

Customer Service

More than any other convenience service, ATMs have been used by adults between the ages of 18 and 39 years for the past three years. Payphones, air hoses, and restrooms make the exception of convenience services above the use of ATMs. There has been a double growth of ATM usage above check cashing services and thrice above money orders in the past couple of years.

With an ATM, your customers stay on your premises and do not go away to withdraw cash from other places.

The latter would mean less time spent by your customers in your location. They are more likely to cut their visits short if they have to go elsewhere to withdraw cash.

Surcharge Revenue

The ATM vault cash provider and the owner usually receive surcharge revenues. This general plan is to attract many potential customers to your machine.

Having 500 people use your ATM monthly at $1.50 in every transaction is better than having 400 people use the device for $2.00. While both cases make a monthly $600 in surcharge revenue, the machine with $1.50 brings in an extra 100 customers monthly. This gives customers thousands of dollars' worth of money.

Benefits on Tax

You can have a lease payment deducted as an operating expense every single month. Leasing, reducing your Alternative Minimum Tax (AMT) and thus enabling you to legally evade tax liability.

Collateral Sales

New income-generating opportunities from ATMs are ever rising. From concert and sporting event tickets, money orders, postage, co-op advertising, to phone cards - all these are new prospects for income that come about every day. Already, there has been a 25% increase in these sales since ATMs took over the job.

Electronic Benefit Transfers (E.B.T)

The subsidy cheque that once came by mail could soon be circulated by electronic means via cards compatible with an ATM.

Higher Retention of Customers

When a business owner allows you to install an ATM in his or her location, he or she is likely to enjoy the benefit of having the capacity to retain customers in the business.

For consumers that do not have a debit card or have an ATM card and are not willing to utilize it at a swipe terminal, the most exclusive method of completing a deal is with cash. With an ATM at their spot, a business owner prevents the occurrence of customers leaving and possibly not coming back to their store.

Generation of Traffic

When an ATM is in an accessible location that is public like a gas station or a lobby of a hotel, it is highly likely to bring about more traffic. When an individual comes in the business to use the ATM, it increases the probability of converting the person into a consumer for other goods or services. When a company strategically positions an ATM in its premises, it draws the client into the store, thus increasing this strategy's success rate.

Increase in Sales

Businesses that are dependent on cash and whose customers continually pay to be in the business place, like lots of bars and entertainment venues, have an ability to make money that is directly linked to the amount of money customer has carried with them.

With an ATM around, the business grants that customer the chance to continue spending money with little or no interference. This does not just allow them to hold on to the customer, but also increase their ordinary level of spending. More so, if the customer is making a withdrawal from an ATM at your business, there is a high probability that he or she will spend money at the business.

Credit Card Fees

It does not cost you anything when a shopper uses an ATM. ATMs do not charge you a transaction fee or a swipe fee. The charges are on the individual withdrawing the money. But, immediately, your customer has cash, he is more inclined to spend it buying an item from you than to use his credit card. This, in turn, reduces both your merchant discount and your swipe fee.

Builds Business Reputation

Businesses that improve convenience to their customers and customer service are considered outstanding in the highly competitive market. Everybody enjoys dealing with companies that care about them, provide answers to their needs and solutions to their problems. When you install an ATM machine in your business space, you are capitalizing on customer service. In that way, you are refining you're the image of your brand in the market.

So you have now decided to have an ATM, have already acquired a location, and have finished installing your ATM. Well, that is not the end of the road for you. You ought to do a bit of marketing as well.

Maybe, you are already enjoying the fruits some increased revenue, but you are not sure if you are receiving the maximum profit that you possibly can from it. You could be looking to find some techniques you can apply to attract more clientele to your ATM, thus accumulating its value to the business.

Well, not to worry. I have brought together a number of significant approaches that can assist in improving the usage of ATMs.

While not every approach is applicable in every company, these tactics below are already proven, with businesses like yours having successfully applied them to bring in more consumers to their ATMs. These kinds of marketing approaches do not cost much. As long as you satisfy your customers' needs and the ATM is convenient.

Growing the Business

To grow your business, you could;

Use your ATMs as mini-billboards.

When a cardholder uses a branded ATM, he or she gets the perception of a wide-ranging availability of ATM. This, therefore, aids in keeping the current customers and gain new ones. ATMs can be a good platform to advertise a certain product. Preferably, a financial institution.

An intriguing and attention-grabbing ATM wrap that has been done professionally could act as a mini ad platform for a financial institution. Besides the income that you will be earning for charging for the space, you will be bringing in both corporate contact with institutions that are essential in the industry, and trust by giving them high visibility and consistency.

A lot can be shown on ATM wraps, from messaging and imagery at the sales-point, as well as logos. This helps to reinforce the brand when customers are contemplating on financial services.

Alter your ATM screens to suit your brand.

Here, you could pass on messages meant for marketing to customers. These messages could include other services provided by financial institutions that you are working with.

Brand the ATMs as it provides leeway to contemporary marketing approaches, which could be used to drive new business and create awareness. When you custom brand ATMs, you may get a chance of earning a soft entry into a market in a geographical region where the business may later increase to with additional branch locations

Give away cash purchase incentives.

This is not a strategy for all businesses. However, if you fancy more customers using your ATM, then try to offer them some kind of reward for using it. Several businesses give away discounts for cash purchases approximately the same as the fees of their credit cards.

Gas stations across the country are a good example of businesses that frequently do this. This strategy gives consumers some motivation to use your ATM. With time, more of them will come.

Customer Care

Customer service is critically significant to your business. It is vital in keeping the customers close to you and getting more worth from them than you possibly can.

In this business, your "customer" can be different types of people.

1. The business owner where your ATM is located
2. The ATM user who withdraws cash
3. The person you sell ATM machines or services to

At a time when businesses are learning to give priority to customer service, your company would crash and burn if it has low levels of customer service. Since most consumers are influenced by a single good experience, one positive experience may be the factor determining their choice to stick with your brand. A negative one, on the other hand, could send them running to your competitor.

Happy Customers

By exhibiting a high standard of customer service, businesses can retain the costs of acquisition of consumers and develop a reliable consumer base that will talk about the business to family and friends. These customers could help in testimonials, case studies, as well as getting reviews from other customers.

When things break, and crisis happens in the company, happy customers are more understanding. They are also less sensitive when prices increase.

For this reason, investing in customer service is very important as it helps propel your business to greater levels. This is one way it helps the company.

When loyal customers are happy and receive good customer service, they spread the word about your brand to others, thus helping you acquire new customers, totally free of charge. When they spread the word, they have more potential for convincing prospective clients to your business. This merits the business more efficiently than your own salespeople and marketing tools can.

In every business, retaining customers is cheaper than acquiring them.

When you increase your rate of customer retention by only 5%, you can liken that to an increase in profit of about 25%. This is because customers who keep coming back to your business are most probably going to spend more on your brand. Studies show that this could go up to exactly 67% more. This later ends in your business cutting down on costs of operations.

When you engage in customer service, you show and build your values, mission, and, most importantly, the image of your brand.

You may know and understand what your brand means and signifies. Nevertheless, your customers cannot know that if you do not let them know. They will interpret all that from your presence on social media, the content you give out, external marketing, and other forms of advertisements.

Happy customers refer others. As mentioned earlier, when customers are happy, they are more likely to tell of the good experience to coworkers, family, and friends.

Actually, according to research by some companies, 77% of customers have told others of positive experiences with the brand. Look at it this way: if you have a fabulous experience, you are most likely to go about raving about it later that night, telling your family about the experience. It is very normal. Though unknowingly, you desire that your loved ones may commit to a brand that you trust can make them happy, too.

Word-of-mouth advertising can be the best form of advertising -- and the cheapest as well. Just give your customers a reason to do it.

Good customer service encourages loyalty from customers. If a customer comes to your business and experiences something, they will have no reason to look elsewhere.

As mentioned earlier, retaining an old consumer is a lot cheaper than acquiring a new one. This essentially means that the longer a customer stays in the business, the more revenue you can expect to generate from the single customer as a company. The longer they stay, the higher your income from them.

Happy Employees

However, your connection to your customers is the customer service team in your company. The team, therefore, has an obligation to represent your brand to the customers effectively.

Without a team doing your customer service, you have no way of maintaining direct contact with your customer. Because of this, it is essential to have a customer service team for them to relay the brand image that you desire your customers to see. They can assist in influencing consumers and convincing them of your strong point over opponents.

Happy customers will come from happy customer service employees.

Every employee would enjoy and feel motivated to come to a workplace where they are appreciated. Otherwise, there would be demotivation and low-performance levels. If anything, 87% of happy employees who are satisfied with their jobs are very enthusiastic about working tremendously hard for the customers of their business. Your customer service team is not left behind in this.

It is essential to note that 55% of employees who strongly feel like they are not happy with their jobs will continue working hard, especially for customers. But, their reason behind serving the customers is about having faith that the customers' lives will improve due to the company's products and services, and wanting to give quality service to the customer.

Their reason for service is mostly about not wanting to get fired before quitting, upholding their integrity and professionalism, receiving acknowledgment from the customers, or being empathetic toward the customers.

For this reason, make your employees feel appreciated and respected if you want them to do their best work. They will then find their own motivation to do a good job deep-down and serve the clients as required, thus leading your consumer to also feel more appreciated and respected.

Invest in a well-trained staff who will be capable of fixing problems, like paper jams, quickly.

When you have a well-trained staff, you:

- Increase the satisfaction of your customers
- Reduce your ATM downtime drastically

- Reduce requests for maintenance from your service provider

It is a chain of reactions. If your customer service team is made up of happy people, they will work extra hard to gratify the needs of the client, as well as exceed the expectations of the consumers.

This goes without a doubt- all your company's staff ought to have good sales and communication skills if you wish to offer the best customer service. You will also be required to display high leadership skills by leading in the provision of exceptional customer service every single time.

How to Make Happy Customers

Building a good relationship with the customer is the key to effective customer service.

Promoting a friendly, helpful, and positive environment as well as showing thanks to the customer will make sure that they leave the premises with a great impression.

Do not be surprised to see the happy customer returning to the premises, or even seeing that they spend more.

To provide the best customer service that customers need:

- Have an idea of what your customers consider to be proper customer service.
- Take your time to research and find out what the customers expect.
- Do a follow-up on both the positive and negative responses you get from the customers and even your customer service team.
- Make sure that you consider providing customer service in all areas of your business.
- Find ways to advance in the level of the customer service you deliver. Do this continuously as tactics keep changing over time.

Your main concern should be to develop a close relationship with your customers. To develop a healthy relationship with your customers, you need to:

- Approach and greet your customers in a natural way that fits that particular situation.
- Express understanding to the customer. Show them that you clearly understand their needs.
- Concentrate on people who are willing to work with your product. Understand and accept that some people will not want your products.
- Offer help to people. For instance, informing a customer about a product or service that you are sure they are usually interested in is very helpful. That can take you a long way in building relationships.
- Keep reminding customers of what they are likely to gain from doing business with you.

Your clientele deserves the best experience as possible from your company.

If clients find the ATM as an inconvenience to them, then it has an unfavorable effect on their relationship with your business.

Handle Complaints Well

Every company is prone to getting complaints from customers. Pay close attention to complaints made by customers. You may discover a thing or two about your product or service that you had no idea about before. Inform your customers that you highly appreciate their feedback.

Refrain from making any objections, as challenging as it may be at times. Keenly listen to what the consumer is complaining about. These factors could be time, merchandise, or price.

Verify how valid each concern is and provide the best solution available.

Know Your Product

Have the features of your product at your fingertips. From their place of manufacture, to the price, to the brand names, as well as where everything is located. The more information about the service or product you have, the more confident you will feel when creating and building your relationship with the customer.

Recognize the features of the products and show the customer how these features can be beneficial to him or her. Make sure that your staff can also extensively explain the feature to the customer.

Blunders to Avoid When Beginning an ATM Business

Now that you have made up your mind to start your own ATM business, below are the mistakes you must avoid so as to ensure the smooth running of the company.

Miscalculating Capital

You will be required to load the machines with cash on a rotational basis. You should count on a weekly amount of about $2,000 per terminal. If your plan is to deploy ten terminals, then this will require you to have a working capital of around $20k or more to service the machines.

Buying Used Equipment

Buying used ATM equipment may seem alluring at the moment, but you ought to be very cautious of the machine that you buy.

It is wise that you should invest in new equipment when commencing an ATM business, considering the EMV regulations nowadays. Purchase a new device to get a 2-year warranty on parts and set your business up for a favorable outcome.

If you acquire old equipment, you may experience problems that may need repairs and possibly lose your spots because of machines running out of service.

Overvaluing Cash Flow

There are many online sources that claim that ATM merchants can make loads of money from each ATM per month. Normally, the estimates made on the sites are way too high.

I recommend that you do your homework extensively and count on an income of $250-$300 on the higher side. A safe bet on the lower side would be $150-$200.

Contact people, get information from several ATM merchants, and keep the ATM income estimates in the business to yourself. There are many companies that can offer you guidance in the right direction on how you can buy ATM machines. They can also help you find locations suitable for your ATM placement.

Establishing Low Margins

When negotiating your commissions and surcharge fees to your merchants, ensure that you practice caution. Do not give away a lot of your margin.

You need to have explicit knowledge of the market and comprehend the requirements. However, do not give away too much of your margins to the merchants.

You will eventually be much happier with future returns if you rate your margins accurately and fairly.

Not Getting a Signed Contract

You must try your best to attain signed agreements with all of your traders, should you think of defending the location of your ATM or selling it.

I have come across various ATM businessmen who operate their ATM businesses short of contracts. So, when the time comes for them to sell the business, the assessment is wind-swept.

Likewise, you will not have anything to stand by if the retailers choose to agree to a competitor coming in or have your ATM removed.

The most important thing is that you get signed contracts. Do vast research on the things you should consider and can do to end up with a good contract.

Service Agreement Mistakes

Creating your service agreement alone from scratch is a bad idea. You will most likely miss something out of the whole process.

Unfortunately, if something wrong happens between you and the owner of the location, then your service agreement will not accurately protect you. It is evident that this can be a terrible idea.

You can still avoid this problem without hiring a lawyer by the use of templates. Through them, you can formulate a service agreement that is custom-made for the situation without missing out on anything.

These service agreement templates will spare you a lot of long-term losses from botched agreements of service and in legal consulting fees.

Therefore, service agreement templates are best done by an ATM processor who would make the completion of the paperwork and getting your ATMs up and running more comfortable and less expensive.

Poor Geographical Placement

When looking for a suitable location, ensure that you do not place your ATMs too far from where you live or each other.

Pick an area carefully and make sure that you hold on to it. The further your spots are from your location, the more the cost of your service and time.

A closely connected range of devices is considerably more appealing to buyers.

Not Establishing a Relationship with a Bank

As an ATM owner, it is wise that you contact a locally recommended bank or your bank, as there are many checkpoints that should be considered.

Make sure that you have a good rapport with them, and they can care for the needs of your ATM business. Do not be surprised to find banks that do not currently assist the ATM industry.

For this reason, ensure that your bank does. There are sites online where you can get assistance on how to find a bank that will give you the support you need in the ATM business. Search for them, contact them, and get the guidance you need to acquire the basic tools to maintain a banking relationship.

Conclusion

Thank you for taking an interest in my book. I hope that it has helped you decide whether you want to enter into a business venture such as this.

I will leave you with a few parting reminders in these final words.

To stand out from the variety of competitors with like products and services, you have to provide more in your company than the thrilling features of your products.

When you provide outstanding customer service, you can be sure to market your company effectively to customers. To build trust, you need loyalty. Customers tend to trust actual human beings more than the values and ideas that a brand offers.

Therefore, through cooperation with your customer service team, your customers may hopefully build relationships with your business that can last a lifetime.

Companies with great customer service have customers willing to pay more. After a positive customer service experience, there is a 50% likelihood that a customer will increase their dealings with a brand.

In reality, 86% of customers would spend up to 25% more money for them to have a better customer service experience. Evidently, customer service is so valuable to customers that they would outright spend more to work together with a brand that does good customer service.

These statistics can definitely not be brushed aside.

One way to provide great customer service is to make sure that your ATM is up and running, safe, and reliable. You will establish your brand of machines as being a local customer favorite.

Losing your ATM uptime may end up with:

- Frustrated, dissatisfied, and unhappy customers
- Loss of surcharge revenue

- Consumers moving their transactions to another business with more convenient ATM service

Carefully choose your vendor. When it comes to choosing a vendor, choose one with experience dealing with your type of ATM. Your service provider should give you a well-trained and experienced operator. They should be quick at responding, quick at resolving issues, as well as making parts available to you.

If you're planning on becoming that operator, ensure that you and your staff obtain adequate training.

Find a service provider with exceptional skills and with a good reputation for providing the best services.

Also, choose a provider that can deal with managed wireless connectivity. This is because your ATM may need a managed wireless connectivity provider in future, to ensure constant uptime.

Connectivity is quite a fundamental part of the functionality of an ATM. For this reason, you will need a servicing partner who can make sure that there is constant quality connectivity.

You need a provider that can provide you with support every hour of every single day. This is so that you can get help for your ATM whenever you need it most - whether day or night.

If this book has assisted or inspired you in any way, would you please consider leaving a review where ever you purchased this book? Reviews help spread the word about books tremendously and will help me reach more people who need help with starting an ATM business for themselves.

Thank you, and I wish you the very best in all of your endeavors.

www.ingramcontent.com/pod-product-compliance
Lightning Source LLC
Chambersburg PA
CBHW071401210526
45465CB00001B/200